W9-CFU-501

EXEMPLARY ELDERS

EXEMPLARY ELDERS

David Levin

THE UNIVERSITY OF GEORGIA PRESS
ATHENS & LONDON

Published by the University of Georgia Press
Athens, Georgia 30602

Designed by Louise M. Jones
Set in 10/13 Galliard
The paper in this book meets the guidelines for permanence and durability of the Committee on Production Guidelines for Book Longevity of the Council on Library Resources.

Printed in the United States of America
94 93 92 91 90 5 4 3 2 1
Library of Congress Cataloging in Publication Data
Levin, David, 1924–
Exemplary elders / David Levin.
p. cm.
ISBN 0-8203-1186-3 (alk. paper)
1. Levin, David, 1924– —Friends and associates.
2. Historians—United States—Biography.
3. Literary historians—United States—Biography.
I. Title.
E175.5.L48A3 1990
973'.07202—dc20 89-5075 CIP
British Library Cataloging in Publication Data available

In memory of
Louis and Rose Braufman Levin

CONTENTS

PREFACE

In 1963, at the Center for Advanced Study in the Behavioral Sciences, I enjoyed the fellowship of several eminent scholars who were already in their mid-fifties, sixties, or seventies. Erik H. Erikson, Meyer Schapiro, Renato Poggioli, Michael Polanyi, Carl Rogers, Lancelot Whyte—what impressed me even more than the achievement of these men, elderly though they seemed to me in my mid-thirties, was their energetic intellectual curiosity. I thought then that if my own mind should survive into the 1980s with even a fraction of the energy that radiated from those elders I would be a lucky man. Their presence set me to thinking once again about the example of elders in my own life, and I decided that I would one day try to characterize the variety and strength of some exemplars.

Readers in the age of Sigmund Freud and Harold Bloom will not uncritically accept Cotton Mather's declaration that they "get more good by objects of their emulation than of their indignation." Nor can the testimony of this book refute Bloom's argument about "the anxiety of influence." Some readers, indeed, will detect evidence of that anxiety in my recognition of defects in several of my elders. But while I recognize both the weakness of hagiography and the power of rebellion as a step toward self-definition, I am convinced that we often underestimate simple encouragement. Written out of love and loyalty, these memoirs do not portray saints, nor should my fond introductory picture of York, Pennsylvania, be read as a nostalgic wish to transform the Great Depression into the Good Old Days. I mean to depict admirable traits or precepts in fallible human beings whose behavior encouraged me, even as late as my mid-fifties, to continue trying to learn how to live.

Five of these elders were public figures, scholars from whom I was deliberately learning about the subjects they professed and whom I knew even in my youth that I was observing as in some more general way exemplary. Even if they had not all, in one way or another, obliged me to reflect on Ralph Waldo Emerson's "The American Scholar," their personalities and the unmistakable self-expression in their work would surely have led me to consider what kind of men they were. I trust that my testimony about them will add to public understanding of their value, but of course I see that the narrator of any memoir becomes a character in his own tale. The peculiarity of my own impressions figures more prominently in the chapters on F. O. Matthiessen, Wallace Stegner, and Samuel Eliot Morison than in those on Perry Miller and Yvor Winters, for I knew Matthiessen, Morison, and Stegner less well.

My other three exemplars, like the people discussed more briefly in the first chapter, were hardly known outside their own small communities. Thomas Weston, Cornelia McLanahan Curtis, and Sarah K. Marker had all lived into their seventies before I began to learn from them about age, about personal loyalty and independence, and about social class. Remembering Weston and Curtis in conjunction with Matthiessen, Morison, and York, Pennsylvania, reminds me, to my surprise, that I still see much of my extracurricular education in the 1940s as an involuntary introduction to the variety of social classes in the United States, and to formal education as a diplomatic passport entitling one to move temporarily among them. I did not seek these people out, but whether one of them introduced me to her guests as "the Harvard professor who is mowing our lawn for the summer" or another took me sailing around Clark's Island in Duxbury Bay, they were teaching me complex, if not always exemplary, social lessons.

I wrote most of this book during my second term as a fellow at the Center for Advanced Study in the Behavioral Sciences, where

I was also preparing an edition of Francis Parkman's nine-volume masterpiece, *France and England in North America*. The center deserves especial gratitude for encouraging not only scholarly but less conventional work. I am also grateful to the University of Virginia for the research leave that enabled me to accept that second fellowship among the behavioral scientists. Early versions of "We're the Team from York, P-A" and "Perry Miller at Harvard" were published in the *Southern Review;* early versions of "Yvor Winters at Stanford" and "To Fight Aloud Is Very Brave," in the *Virginia Quarterly Review;* an early version of "Samuel Eliot Morison," in the *Sewanee Review*.

Many friends and colleagues, both elders and juniors, have helped me by reading all or part of this manuscript. Robert D. Cross and Alan B. Howard have read it more than once, and I am grateful for both their generous patience and their editorial acuteness. Among others who read the entire manuscript, W. W. Abbot, Douglas Anderson, Stephen Arch, Malcolm Call, Janice Carlisle, James M. Cox, Brock Dethier, Paul John Eakin, Melody Graulich, Patricia M. Levin, the late Gary H. Lindberg, Thomas Moser, B. L. Reid, and Philip Winsor gave me valuable suggestions. J. C. Levenson read original and revised drafts of the chapters on F. O. Matthiessen and Samuel Eliot Morison, and he not only corrected some of my errors about both mentors but also provided facts and insights that helped me to understand them better. George Core, Leo Marx, and the late John Lydenberg corrected errors in the chapters on Matthiessen and Morison. Patrick Flynn of the Massachusetts Historical Society refreshed my inaccurate memory about the Paul Revere Liberty Bowl. Monroe Levin and Richard Smyser corrected some of my erroneous memories of York, Pennsylvania.

WE'RE THE TEAM FROM YORK, P-A

AMERICAN HISTORY IN A JEWISH CHILDHOOD

Philip Roth's *The Ghost Writer* (1979) reinforces an assumption that is shared by a number of Jewish writers who disagree with Roth on other subjects as vehemently as they do with one another. Roth, Alfred Kazin, Saul Bellow, Bernard Malamud, and Norman Podhoretz all ask their readers to assume that American Jews born between 1910 and 1940 grew up in Jewish neighborhoods in big cities and discovered gentile American history as outsiders, attached in only the most casual ways to particular places or local traditions. My own experience cannot invalidate those assumptions, but in meditating on the American past that I have been studying for forty years, I find myself unable to affirm them. My brothers and sisters, our nearest Jewish friends, and I were all closely identified with a small historic city.

I was born in York, Pennsylvania, in 1924, the third son (followed by two daughters) of parents who had escaped Boston Road and the Bronx. One of my earliest mementos is the silver medal my father won in 1912 by declaiming Patrick Henry's most famous speech in a contest at the DeWitt Clinton High School. One of my oldest sentimental tales recounts my father's withdrawal from DeWitt Clinton to support his parents, brothers, and sister with a weekly salary of six dollars. Opportunity came to him later, in the Algerine form of a job managing a new clothing store in Kankakee, Illinois, when he was only nineteen. He loved to tell us children that the man who interviewed him in a

New York hotel for that position had advised him not to respond so promptly if he should ever be paged again: "Let the bellhop call your name throughout the lobby, and then identify yourself casually, as if you were accustomed to the publicity." Our father also enjoyed showing us the brown clipping in which a Kankakee reporter had described our mother's daring elopement from New York to Kankakee when she was only eighteen, and he had a scrapbook of other brown clippings about meetings of a Bronx social club which had invariably included Louis Levin's baritone solo. He was not assimilated, but he was not alienated.

Other assignments had taken my parents to manage stores in Troy, New York; in Easton and Reading, Pennsylvania; and at last in York, where they soon went into business for themselves and then stayed for the remaining thirty-five years of my father's life. A few months before my birth they moved into the new suburban house in which the five children grew up. This was in an unincorporated neighborhood of about 150 houses, called East York.

In the years since I left York for college, I have often been reminded that our indoctrination in loyalty to the home town was extraordinarily effective—the more extraordinary because we were well aware of our distinctive heritage. We were the children of an immigrant mother (brought from Rumania as a child by her young parents), and the grandchildren of four immigrants who had fled Russia or Rumania. Our parents did not teach us Yiddish but spoke it to each other occasionally when they wanted us not to understand. Our father had founded the York Jewish Community Center (later the YMHA), and throughout our childhood we had complicated ties with both the Orthodox synagogue and the Reform temple. All three sons studied Hebrew with the Orthodox rabbi after school, several days a week for two or three years before the bar mitzvah. I can remember that the last three months of my own three years' training in Hebrew were especially separate from the normal life of my classmates, because I had entered the ninth grade that autumn and was newly enrolled in the large Phineas Davis Junior High School (named, I took some local pride in knowing, for an early builder of locomotives in the town we had learned to call York, P-A). Preoccupied with the bar mitzvah, I had no time that autumn for the new opportunities in sports and drama.

Throughout the thirties, moreover, we were aware of nazism as well as Father Coughlin and domestic forms of anti-Semitism. I was nine when Hitler came to power, and eleven when the first refugees from Germany began to arrive in York. During my first year or two in Hebrew school, I became intensely pious, under the hearty influence of our Talmud Torah teacher, Rabbi Moses Friedman, who encouraged us to feel proud of our ten-cent weekly contributions to a fund for planting trees in Eretz Yisroel; proud, too, of the beautiful prayers we were learning to chant. Surely my own strenuous and all too visible piety had at least one or two roots in other kinds of pride, for in our household no prayers were spoken. The sabbath candles, over which my mother waved her hands and prayed inaudibly, were the only vestiges of her Orthodox upbringing. My father acted energetically as president of the Jewish Community Center and B'nai B'rith, but he could not read Hebrew and did not attend either synagogue except for the rites of passage in his children's lives. I remember feeling that my resolution to obey Mosaic law came in response to Rabbi Friedman's lucid teaching, but I must have perceived as well that walking several miles to the synagogue, and spending the Passover week with an Orthodox family who lived near the *shul,* were challenging ways for a middle child to get more attention than I had won by emulating my older brothers' academic distinction.

It is these complex and pervasive marks of separateness that make our local patriotism seem now to have been extraordinarily vigorous. Friends who grew up in suburbs of Chicago, Boston, New York, Philadelphia tell me they had no strong feelings of identification with the home town. Why did we, with all our separating influences, feel so closely attached to the place and its past? We lived in three social worlds: our neighborhood and its fine public school; the Jewish Community Center in town, with its

Talmud Torah and its informal ties to the Orthodox synagogue; and the temple. Membership in the temple overlapped with our associations in the Hebrew school, since my brothers and many of the boys in Reform families went through both the bar mitzvah ceremony in the *shul* and the confirmation a year later in the temple. We did not learn until long afterward that a few neighbors had expressed anxious displeasure when our parents had become the first Jews in the neighborhood, but we did know every one of the children in the six other Jewish families scattered through East York, and even within the neighborhood we had special friendships with some of those Jewish children. Both in East York and in the city, our parents had only Jewish friends. Their respectful and even generous relationship with other neighbors and with parents of our gentile schoolmates never warmed into friendship. These neighbors and our parents seemed to have agreed tacitly that real friendships would begin with our generation.

Both in the neighborhood and in the city, we children had two sets of friends. Some of the Jewish friends, of course, had their own relationship to the mixed group, but others we saw in situations that only rarely included any children who were not Jewish. My nearest brother and I, for example, spent many summer days and weeks in elaborate and protracted competition with two other pairs of Jewish brothers, the Millers and the Oppenheimers. For a few weeks one summer, we played poker, Monopoly, Parcheesi, Hearts, and Blackjack in the Oppenheimers' garage. I don't remember that any of our gentile friends ever risked their pennies in Oppenheimer's Gambling Joint, but the Miller brothers and I spent hundreds of hours playing baseball and football in pick-up games with fifteen or twenty non-Jewish boys, and for at least two summers we helped to organize East York teams to play a series of games against rivals from a subdivision called Elmwood. We knew that York was the city of the White Roses and that its archrival in every sport was some amateur or professional team of Red Roses from Lancaster, across the Susquehanna River. We gave our rivalry with Elmwood the same intense significance, which was magnified by the formal setting. We played these games not on the vacant lots in East York but on Victory Diamond, a full-sized baseball field owned by the Victory Fire Department, with an actual pitcher's mound and rubber, a home plate built into the ground, and (sometimes) regulation bases.

It was in these games that we first saw Charley White, a fine pitcher who threw intimidating roundhouse curves that too often broke over the plate for strikes. We tried unsuccessfully to upset him by calling him Whitey-without-a-shirt, because he was the only shirtless player on either team. I did not know, when he was spinning those curves past our bats, that he would become my close friend from the time we met again on the high school tennis team until he died in a military plane crash during the Second World War. (I was in the army air force at the time. When my father sent me the news article reporting Charley's death, he reminded me that my parents still had a pair of Charley's pajamas, for the times he would decide to stay in our house overnight.) I remember now that he was the only non-Jewish guest, except for one friend of my brother's, who frequented our house. Our friendships with other neighbors and classmates often led us to their houses but seldom brought them to ours.

Against our ecumenical games on Victory Diamond I can set the Sunday morning baseball games at Eagle Park, the professional White Roses' home diamond, which the Jewish Community Center regularly leased for informal games among the men, as it later leased the basketball court of the Methodist church on winter evenings. Some of my happiest memories recall the joy of being allowed to enter the Sunday baseball game as a pinch runner for my father. But even while these segregated games were going on every week, my enterprising brother and his indefatigably resourceful Lutheran partner, Dick Smyser, projected schemes that drew the attention of the whole neighborhood. The most ambitious and successful of these were a nightclub, the Barcelona, which lived in splendor for one glorious night on the large verandah of the Methodist Schimmels; and a grammar school newspaper, to whose editorship Dan Meckley and I succeeded after the founders had moved on to junior high school.

On our quiet street, too, my father and Jesse Chock, a Jewish neighbor whom we all called Uncle Jesse, performed rituals that had a national and historical significance. From the time I was five or six, wearing gloves as big as my forearm, my father sponsored boxing matches on our lawn, and he and Uncle Jesse led slow-pitch baseball games in Keesey Street, with all the boys on the street participating. It was Uncle Jesse who made the Fourth of July delightfully memorable during those Depression years. He managed a pajama factory in town, and we all knew that he went to work at six o'clock in the morning. At six o'clock on any summer evening we could walk down Keesey Street and hear him embellishing "My Walking Stick" or some other tune with the heavy rolling chords and the stridently repetitive echoes of the early Irving Berlin. (One of the first signs of my brother's virtuosity was his hilarious mimicry of the Uncle Jesse sound.) A few minutes later we would see and sometimes hear Uncle Jesse napping sonorously in his wing chair. But on the Fourth of July he lit up Keesey Street with rockets, roman candles, and pinwheels. Although I assume that other neighbors contributed to the supply, it is possible that only Uncle Jesse's prosperity and generosity could afford the display. His fat silhouette is the one that dominates my memory of those splendid nights, as it must loom in the minds of other survivors both Jewish and gentile. In the light of the last roman candle, that uniquely triangular stomach would stand out, with the belt on the trousers magically horizontal, girdling the very apex of the triangle even as Uncle Jesse dipped gracefully, in a kind of curtsy, to light a skyrocket. Behind him, on the dark verandah across the street, Dr. C. B. Heinly, principal of the high school, watched the flamboyant displays in benignly aloof dignity.

It was the schools, and especially the Hiestand Grammar School, that tied us most securely to the local past. At Hiestand we soon learned the significance of the names among which we lived. York County had first been settled in the 1730s and 1740s by German pietists who were also refugees. Three of the four teachers in Hiestand were Lutherans named Kauffman, Hirsch, and Schroeder, and our neighbors included Saltzgivers, Auspitzes, Dittenhafers, Obermaiers, Schimmels, Yoders, Rudisills, Meckleys, Geeseys, Greenawalts, Shadles, Sipes, Loucksses, Getzes, Sowerses, Smysers, and Lauers. In high school we would befriend Oberdicks, Oelwilers, Flinchbaughs, Grosses, Lutzes, and Pfaltzgraffs. Most of the children we knew were Lutherans, but some Mennonites and Dunkers attended our schools. We had our Talmud Torah, and all these groups had their Bible schools for several weeks in summer, and special training at times during the school year. Some of the friends were committed after school to combined religious and athletic programs at the YMCA. When I was ten, the YMHA rented the Boy Scouts' summer camp for one week, and my eleven-year-old brother and I thus came to know the same campground as some of our gentile friends.

In this context our acceptance of the local past was not genealogical but ideological and spiritual. We knew about pluralism before we knew its name—before we heard of James Fenimore Cooper's polyglot pioneers and before Oscar Handlin wrote *The Uprooted*. Long before we attended the senior high school in town, we knew that it had been named for William Penn, and that religious liberty and brotherly love had been associated with his name and with our commonwealth for more than two centuries. I don't remember that we ever explicitly recognized a parallel between our own religious separateness and that of the founding Dunkers and Mennonites, but we certainly perceived that we were not the only religious group whose principles sometimes conflicted with practices in the school or the community. We knew Seventh Day Adventists as well as Jehovah's Witnesses. We happily pledged allegiance to the flag every morning, recited the prayer that Christians called the Lord's, and took our turns at reading the Old Testament passage from the Bible. Our teachers discreetly assigned the New Testament verses to others. My brother, the best pianist in the school, played the hymns that we all sang at the beginning of the school day, and without any struggle or embarrassment I sang selectively with the others.

I never heard of any parental protest against these daily rituals in the public schools. Not until I studied the flag-salute cases in a college course in constitutional law did it occur to me that we had regularly violated the First Amendment. I would sing all the nontrinitarian words (except *God*) to "Faith of Our Fathers" or "O God, Our Help in Ages Past," but would hum or otherwise slur the trinitarian lines. Since we were learning to chant "Kadosh, kadosh, kadosh" in the Hebrew school, I would sing "Holy, Holy, Holy" in the public schools, but not the resounding last lines of the refrain: "God in three persons, blessed Trinity."

We joined with our Lutheran schoolmates, then, in laughing at the strange locutions of the Pennsylvania Dutch, the Pennsylwania weterans who went down into the walley and fired wolley after wolley but in wain. On Sunday evening our whole family sat by the Silvertone radio to enjoy the latest hilarious instance of Jack Benny's stinginess and the ethnic accents of Mrs. Nussbaum on the Fred Allen show. We laughed affectionately, too, at the accent of our own Norman Freireich, who in the name of the congregation gave every bar mitzvah boy a certificate which he called a stiffticket, and who always gave the same admonition as he presented an inscribed Bible: "Take it don from the shelf once in a while, it shouldn't get dosty." But we knew that dungeon, fire, and sword had actually been used against the Mennonites and Dunkers as well as the Jews, and that our presence in the schools expressed faith in the American future as well as respect for the best ideals of the American past. The boosting vanity of a local businessman who bought uniforms for the entire high school band bought him the privilege of having his own song adopted by the school: "We're from York, We're from York, We're the team from York, Peeeeaay." That boosting spirit also tied our local pride to the Articles of Confederation, which had been drafted while the Continental Congress, having crossed the Susquehanna River to escape the English armies, had met in York for ten months.

I can still hear the voice of a new boy in the Hiestand School, the first southern accent I had ever heard in real life, intoning the sacred local facts when Mr. Kauffman called on him for the first time in class: "From *Sep*tembah, *Sev*enteen *Sev*enty-seven to June, *Sev*enteen *Sev*enty-eight, the *Cahn*tinental *Cahn*gress sat in Yawk, Pehnsylvayniah."

So far as I can tell even now, the community's emphasis on its brief Revolutionary glory was no more genealogical than our own vicarious participation. There were annual reunions of Smysers or Stambaughs at Farquhar Park, and I remember that one or two of these gathered in so many relatives that only the county fairground was large enough for the picnic. Perhaps because there had been few local heroes of the kind that abounded in Philadelphia, Boston, and Virginia, what we learned about the place concerned events and qualities rather than families: not only the Articles of Confederation but the exposure of the Conway Cabal, a plot to oust George Washington as commander-in-chief.

We were also taught that in its rich soil York County had a remarkably diversified agriculture, the city of York an unusually diversified group of industries and (appropriately, according to our pluralistic faith) an extraordinary number and range of churches. Somehow the discovery of these welcome truths has always been pleasantly associated in my mind with the happy news, which I also learned in the Hiestand School, that Pennsylvania was the Keystone State, essential to the arch formed by the original thirteen. When I read in 1979 that the nuclear accident at Three Mile Island might have contaminated the dairy farms of York County, I felt the more indignant because it was my rich native soil that was threatened. The Kempers' farm, from which we annually took dried ears of field corn for our Halloween raids on neighborhood windows, had long since been replaced by suburban houses, some of which my own father built after World War II. But I still feel closely attached to the dairy farms and strongly moved to defend the quality of that soil. Although I now recognize that I needed to feel a sense of belonging, both in our large family and in the neighborhood, it is the community's encouragement of our attachment to its present and past that deserves especial emphasis.

Of course the Daughters of the American Revolution must have had local members, for they sponsored an annual essay contest at William Penn, but until the national organization refused to allow Marian Anderson, the black singer, to give a concert in Constitution Hall, I knew about the DAR only as the sponsor of the contest that my oldest brother had won with an essay on Benjamin Franklin. President Roosevelt's wife had resigned from the DAR after the Anderson incident in the year before my own class competed for the DAR prize. The assigned topic in our year was Thomas Paine. None of the local Daughters objected to the celebrity of Howard Fast's *Citizen Tom Paine* two years afterward, although Eleanor Roosevelt was to be castigated during the 1950s for having invited the left-wing novelist to the White House. My essay on Paine won nothing, but I was cheered by his insistence in 1776 on the diverse origins of Pennsylvania's citizens. Surely my inclination to read Benjamin Franklin sympathetically had its origin in my brother's experience as well as in the emphasis that our earliest educational experience put upon equal opportunity and the Revolutionary glory of early Pennsylvania. My sister tells me that she knew of some plaintive whispering when she became the first Jew to win the American Legion award for good citizenship, in the year of her graduation from Hiestand, and that she heard similar grumbling when she won a scholarship to Bryn Mawr, but such honors were open to us all.

What we were learning in school about free opportunity was borne out in our parents' life and in our own, even when we were not concerned with patriotic subjects. Although they had lost the small fortune that they had accumulated in the 1920s, our parents managed to hold on to their house. They hung on to their retail clothing store for a year or two, long after their 1926 seven-passenger Cadillac had been shut up in our garage because they couldn't afford to run it, and then our father tried for several years to support us as an agent for the New York Life Insurance

Company. At forty, a year after his first heart attack, he opened a real estate office and began to earn enough to repay some of his debts. During all those years both our parents persisted in regarding York as their refuge in the land of opportunity. As one after another of *their* parents died in New York during the thirties, our parents often reminded us of the contrast between crowded New York apartments or streets and the open air, pleasant lawns, and broad, empty, tree-lined streets of East York. Our father was baffled by his mother's preference for the hot, crowded city she knew, and by her inability to sleep in the silence of our neighborhood.

Our elementary school had four rooms for its eight grades, and a total enrollment of about 120. Throughout my years there, each class of about 15 pupils studied quietly in alternate hours while the teacher taught the other class seated in the same room. Our teachers were happier in the alternate years when my brother was in third, fifth, and seventh grade; only in his odd-numbered years could my intense competition with him be restricted to the daily softball games at recess and noon, and to the spelling bees in the weeks before the county's spelling contest. But of course I observed his achievement and learned by his example. We were expected to represent the school in the annual spelling contest at the York County Courthouse, and in the semiannual programs in December and May. I remember playing Scrooge in a program staged by Hiestand, which had no auditorium, in the neighborhood's Lutheran church. In junior and senior high school, too, I performed, as my brothers had done, in plays with titles like *The Phantom Tiger, Everyman,* and *You Can't Take It with You*. Since my brothers had prepared the way, my prevailing recollection is the pleasure of being welcomed and encouraged at each stage by teachers who seemed genuinely glad to meet apt, interested students.

The debating team, the dramatic club, debating clubs; English, French, and Latin classes; the *York High Weekly*—all encouraged us to believe not only that all doors to achievement were open but also that we could enter them all at once. I was less surprised than

I should have been when the varsity tennis coach invited me to try out for the team, and more resentful than I should have been when the *Weekly*'s faculty adviser objected to my efforts to achieve even more versatility than my brothers.

The high school in those last years before World War II was still for a majority of students the last stage of formal education. The literary and debating societies resembled college fraternities and sororities, with social as well as intellectual criteria for admission and with ritualistic, hazing initiations. But the social criteria emphasized "popularity" rather than religion or family. Jews were admitted to all four of the leading clubs, although many more Jewish boys joined the Alpha Debating Society than its competitor, the Demosthenian Literary Society. The people quietly excluded were those who had chosen to enter the commercial or vocational programs rather than the old classical (in my day the college preparatory) curriculum. The less social clubs—Latin, French, Spanish, German, Mathematics, Thespians—were open to anyone interested in the subject.

I don't remember wondering why there were no black students in the Hiestand Grammar School. After black students did appear in our secondary-school classes, I too easily explained their absence from the literary clubs and, with rare exceptions, the college preparatory classes by a cursory, neatly circular determinism: living in poor neighborhoods, they had gone to the weaker elementary schools, and now they were preparing to work, in jobs that would help them support their parents, brothers, and sisters. Not until I read *Native Son* in 1940, after my junior year in high school, did I begin to see the strength of the connections among various kinds of discrimination.

For our family the Depression too was certainly real, but we younger children saw its effects in relatively minor ways. The pennies that I ventured in Oppenheimer's Gambling Joint came from my earnings as a mower of lawns and a deliverer of *Liberty* and other McFadden magazines. From the age of ten onward, I had to earn all my spending money, to wear clothes and a baseball glove handed down from my oldest brother, and to wait my turn—the year that my middle brother left the junior high school as I entered it—to have the family bicycle for my own three-mile round trip to school. We children were always aware of the recurrent crises, but we always had abundant food. Even our oldest brother, who had to drop out of Penn State for a year to run the real estate office after our father's second heart attack, had the satisfaction of knowing that he was the first in the whole line to attend a residential college and that the whole family was committed to his eventual establishment as a lawyer. When the high school tennis coach, a Harvard graduate who was also an English teacher, insisted that I apply to Harvard College, I was able to borrow the money for my first-term bill from a close friend of my parents.

That admirable friend, Henry Erdos, was exemplary for more than his loyal generosity. He was a Hungarian Jew who had been drafted into the Austro-Hungarian army during World War I and had emigrated after the Armistice. By the time I went to him for help, he had become manager of the Triumph Hosiery mill in York, and after the Second World War he became president of Danskin. As he grew wealthy neither he nor the similarly wealthy Uncle Jesse Chock moved out of East York. Both had lived in semidetached houses in my early childhood. Both moved just a few hundred yards to larger though not ostentatious houses. They continued to live among neighbors who walked several miles to their daily work or rode the bus: Earl Saltzgiver, window dresser in a department store, who owned no "machine" and rode the bus; Daniel Meckley, my classmate's father, whose precisely timed walk home from the Weaver piano factory would have let us set our watches accurately every afternoon, if we had had watches. Kenny Mundis, who lived around the corner from us, joined the Civilian Conservation Corps. Yet Stewart Lauer, who lived on our block, was president of the York Corporation, the largest industrial firm in the city. The Wagenbergs and Reichers, the two Jewish refugee families that settled in our neighborhood in the mid-1930s, had enough money to buy their houses and open a business, and were thus better off than most refugees, but their acceptance in East York and in the marketplace confirmed my belief that York was a genuine refuge in the land of opportunity.

In this context of economic, ethnic, and religious pluralism our experience of domestic anti-Semitism did not weaken our sense of participation in more affirmative American traditions. We took pride in the home runs of the Philadelphia Phillies' Chuck Klein (learning only years afterward that he was not Jewish) and the Detroit Tigers' Hank Greenberg, in the touchdowns of Marshall Goldberg at Pitt, and in the heavyweight boxing championship of Max Baer. We knew that the York Country Club and some residential areas excluded Jews, that friendships with gentile girls among our schoolmates might be forbidden or arbitrarily terminated by their parents, and that our own parents disapproved of such friendships. Several times during my years at Hiestand, the roughhousing after a late-afternoon football game or during an evening of Halloween pranks brought anti-Semitic epithets about my ears. My relationship with the most vociferous offenders was never easy thereafter, but the same group that so rarely permitted thoughtless teasing to take this vicious form treated me heartily as a comrade through years of play and study. Far more baffling was the insensitivity of an English teacher at Phineas Davis who managed in 1937–38 to teach *Ivanhoe, The Talisman, The Merchant of Venice,* and *Oliver Twist* without ever questioning or analyzing the literary practice of referring to a villain as "the Jew."

Throughout the thirties images of Hitler and Mussolini dominated my picture of modern European history. I don't remember that Stalin figured in the picture until after his troops had invaded Finland. My parents and their friends often spent evenings discussing the developing crisis, the growing power of anti-Semitism. What I remember from their discussions of the Spanish Civil War, for example, is the ominous evidence of Hitler's power rather than any ideological contrast of fascism and communism. From the time of Mussolini's invasion of Ethiopia, at least some of our teachers complemented the general welcome that I felt, by volunteering their own agreement with what my parents were saying about the assassination of Dolfuss, the invasion of Austria and Czechoslovakia. Long before war actually began in Poland, I had connected images of German soldiers in World War I movies with a foreboding that Hitler's storm troopers, the dive bombers at Guernica, the older and more modern submarines would one day be at war with the United States. I remember that when France fell during the spring of my junior year, Lambert Greenawalt passionately condemned Hitler for half an hour in an English class on *Macbeth*. Thirty years later, when invited to teach at the University of Virginia, I first thought not of Thomas Jefferson but of Franklin D. Roosevelt; I had first heard of Charlottesville in 1940, as the place from which FDR broadcast his denunciation of Mussolini's stab in the back of France. In that context my identification of American democratic tradition with the ancient pluralism of York County and the defense of parliamentary liberty against nazism would have flourished even if the teacher of our required course in American history had not been a Jewish veteran of World War I.

Mr. Trattner, our history teacher, was the nephew of Abe Trattner, whom we had all known from our earliest years as the patriarch of our Jewish community, beloved founder of the *shul*. By the time I was a student in the Talmud Torah, our reverence for Abe Trattner was often qualified by our nudges and snickers as his irrepressible belches resounded through the synagogue, but we did revere him. He had come to York in 1883, before any of my grandparents had even thought of emigrating. During my high school years his nephew Norman, the history teacher, already an active member of the Veterans of Foreign Wars, founded the Jewish War Veterans. Norman's way of resisting anti-Semitism in 1940 was to publicize the patriotic service of Jews, and although his heavily didactic method was sometimes embarrassing, I enjoyed his insistence in our history class that a Jewish sailor had played an important part in Columbus's first voyage, and that Haym Solomon had distinguished himself as a financier of the Revolution. I was glad to have my classmates hear this ethnic confirmation that many other circumstances of my childhood had already established firmly in my mind.

At Harvard, of course, I eventually learned that many of the influences encouraging young scholars to study American history and literature had nothing to do with the peculiar conditions of York, Pennsylvania. Both before and after the war interrupted our training, my classmates from Jewish and non-Jewish families in Minneapolis, Brookline, Cleveland, Lawrence, Springfield, New York, and Charlotte were caught up in the exhilarating proliferation of American studies. Surely it was the example of Professors Perry Miller, Matthiessen, Morison, Schlesinger, Merk, Handlin, and H. M. Jones, as much as any peculiarities of our home towns, that drew many of us into graduate study in Harvard's American civilization program. Surely too, our sense of growing possibilities owed much to the country's new status as a superpower, whether or not we thought the country was likely to fulfill the unredeemed promises about which I was then learning more than I had ever known in York. But as I concentrated my research on George Bancroft, John Lothrop Motley, and other contemporaries of Emerson and Cooper, I found surprising confirmation (despite their weakness for Teutonic germs) of the pluralistic faith that I had learned in York. And when my studies with Perry Miller and Samuel Eliot Morison led me into seventeenth-century New England, I was fascinated not only by the Puritans' study of the Torah, but also by their insistence on their spiritual, nongenealogical descent from Abraham. Their intolerance was notorious, but they said they had escaped the English pharaoh and had crossed deeper waters than the Red Sea, hoping to transform the American wilderness into the New Jerusalem. For them William Bradford and John Winthrop were antitypes of Moses, and for me as well as others Bradford's history *Of Plymouth Plantation* was an eloquent monument to all immigrants. I did not know then that I would write the biography of a pious child named Cotton Mather, who had taken pride in fetching gold "out of the dunghills of the Talmud," but I was pleased to see that the tough-minded refugees called Puritans had long ago set a precedent for the kind of ideological inheritance that had made me feel at home in York.

Perry Miller

Rarely have I felt so pervasive a sense of a community's exhilaration as in the atmosphere at Harvard during the first weeks of February 1946. The war, of course, had ended in mid-August, but the big wave of returning veterans did not reach Cambridge until the beginning of the spring semester. Several thousand of us rejoiced not only in the victory but in our survival, our liberation, our return to scholarship. Most of us had left Harvard before the Allies had established so much as a beachhead on the European mainland, and before the tide in the Pacific had turned against Japan. Although the two to five years of our military service had often seemed interminable, the transformation from grim resistance to total victory now seemed to have been accomplished with amazing speed. Many of us knew that the costs had been unspeakably terrible, but many more seemed to believe that all things—except finding a one- or two-bedroom apartment in Cambridge—were possible. Scholarship would flourish. The United Nations might keep the peace. The civilian economy might be rehabilitated, Europe's cities rebuilt, a homeland secured for the survivors of the Holocaust, Japan transformed into a democratic state, atomic energy applied to human benefit.

To those of us who were still undergraduates concentrating in history and literature, the sense of community was intensified by the participation of several academic generations. Captain Samuel Eliot Morison, President Roosevelt's personal nominee to write the history of United States naval operations in World War II, and Major Perry Miller, who as an officer in the OSS had accompanied the French hero General Leclerc in his triumphant sweep to liberate Alsace, were both lecturing on early American culture. Some veterans rolled their eyes when Morison appeared for his first lecture in his naval uniform, set his cap down precisely with its bill pointed ninety degrees to the audience's left, and suggested that the students wearing open shirts and sweaters adopt the traditional dress of Harvard gentlemen and scholars, a necktie and a sports jacket. Some groaned during one of Miller's lectures later on in the term when, having called Thomas Paine an expert on psychological warfare, Miller appealed to his own authority as a psychological warfare *officer*. But our respect for the historical imagination of these great teachers, our belief in its relevance to modern American life, and our eagerness to join them in the common enterprise of scholarship were surely reinforced by our belief that they had participated with us in the war against the Axis.

Because the war had cost us from two to five years, the mingling of students from different academic generations intensified our feeling that we formed a community of scholars. Since I had married during the war and was no longer eligible to live in Lowell House, I had almost no occasion to meet younger classmates, but the tutorial system gave at least some of them the same opportunities we veteran undergraduates had to meet graduate students and professors. Enrolled with us in some of the classes designated for advanced undergraduates and graduate students were a number of the best teaching fellows who already were or would soon become our tutors. In Perry Miller's famous course "Romanticism in American Literature" or F. O. Matthiessen's "Twentieth-Century American Poetry," both given in the summer of 1946, Laurence Holland, J. C. Levenson, and Leo Marx were all enrolled after they had already been appointed teaching fellows for the coming year. And these Ivy Leaguers were joined by a new group of outsiders. Sherman Paul of Iowa was in one class, along with Merrill Peterson of Kansas. In Matthiessen's course that summer, we even wondered at the brashness of a stocky, square-faced young man who was reputed to be a doctor of philosophy. When he stood at the back of the crowded room and jabbed his finger at the air between himself and the podium, I did not know that his name was Leslie Fiedler, that he was already on the faculty of the University of Montana, or that he had not invented the axiom he uttered: "A poem must not mean but be."

The joy of our return was so exhilarating that (at least as my memory now insists) we were not downcast by unpleasant living conditions. Married in the summer of 1945, Pat Marker and I had lived first in a motel in Albuquerque and then in a bedroom, sharing the bath with six other couples, in a house in Topeka, Kansas. On my return to Harvard we had been lucky enough to find two rooms in a house on the downhill side of Buena Vista Park, near Porter Square, where we had no vista at all but were determined to work out a reasonable schedule for sharing the kitchen and bath with the couple who rented us the rooms. What finally drove us out of that house in mid-April was not the landlord or landlady but her aging father. Trying to study in our sitting room, in one of the wicker chairs, I could wear warm slippers to insulate my feet from the linoleum carpet; I learned to ignore the jars of ostrich eggs on the bookshelves, and the landlady's high school diploma (with typing certificate tucked into the lower left-hand corner) on the wall beside the photograph of a Labrador retriever. It was old Mr. Langille's deafness that blasted us out. He had to turn the volume so high that when he listened to the Answer Man ("How many bones has the pterosaur?"), I found myself waiting for the booming answer instead of attending to my book. But even as we strove to find an apartment of our own we knew that other married students were commuting from prefabricated apartments Harvard had reserved at Fort Devens, thirty or forty miles away. And when we were swindled by a confidence-man who sublet his apartment to us and to ten other couples, spending all our advance deposits before two of the couples insisted on moving in rather than accept a second postponement,

Pat and I were glad that our prudent landlady had decided after the first postponement that she wouldn't advertise our rooms until we had actually moved out. I was also grateful to have the GI Bill's benefits and the support of Pat, who had already graduated from the College of Wooster. Those two sources of funds enabled me to be a full-time student rather than work from twenty to forty hours a week for my room and board, as I had done before the war.

Pat, like scores of other wives of returning veterans, had to find a job months before we could find an apartment of our own. Curtiss-Wright had sent her and many other women to the University of Minnesota to study aeronautical engineering in 1943, and she had worked in the Curtiss-Wright plant in Columbus for a year. Now she went to work as a draftsman in a small company in Cambridge called Photoswitch. Although the chief executive officer was a woman, Pat sat next to a man who earned two dollars and seventy-five cents an hour by doing precisely the same work for which Pat was paid one dollar. But with the ninety dollars (besides books and tuition) that the federal government paid me every month, we thought we were reasonably well off. As we met several of my old friends and a few of her own, at Wooster alumni meetings and through the Weston family (who will figure in chapter 5), Pat shared the community's exhilaration. As it had done during the war, the staid old university was trying to adjust to novel conditions—the presence not only of hundreds of veterans alongside the usual undergraduates, but also of wives and children. By June Pat had found more congenial employment at the Wright Brothers Wind Tunnel at the Massachusetts Institute of Technology, and at last we were settled in a decent apartment in Brighton. Not until the spring of 1948 did the visits of a persistent rat to our pantry and the battles in a husband-battering family next door impel us to move once again.

In that first week of February 1946 I found myself happily enrolled in the classes of three professors who had also just returned from the wars: Miller, Morison, and Albert J. Guerard, for whom I was bound to turn out a one-thousand-word short story every week. I do not remember feeling any surprise at my first sight of the decor in Perry Miller's suite in Leverett House, less than a week after Captain Morison had worn his uniform to class. Miller lounged in an easy chair, his long legs crossed. He rose to shake my hand when I informed him that he had been assigned as my tutor in history and literature, and he invited me to sit in a black wooden chair with cherry arms and the Harvard seal on the back. As I took my seat I had to notice that a German battle flag, with an immense swastika, hung on the wall behind me and that a pair of knee-high boots gleamed beside the left rear leg of my chair. "I got the flag and the boots when I liberated Strasbourg with Leclerc," Miller said, laughing away the bravado in his reduction of Leclerc's role. "Where were you?"

That was the simplest question he ever asked me. For the next fourteen weeks I often felt as if, having been captured by the Germans after all, I were under interrogation in front of that flag. Miller was not unkind; he was simply relentless, and he was often as indirect as Dostoyevsky's Porfiry Petrovich. The hour would begin with my reading of a four- or five-page paper I had written about the book he had assigned during our last meeting, and then the interrogation would begin as the light from his floor lamp shone on his prematurely white hair (he was only forty-one) and glanced off his rimless spectacles. I remember an intense session that must have lasted only a few minutes, although it still seems to have been much longer. He wanted me to discuss the importance of Darwinism in *The Education of Henry Adams,* but he began the questioning by asking only this: "Whom had Adams been reading before he wrote *The Education?*" I knew that R. W. Emerson, whom we had discussed just seven days ago, was not the right answer, although Emerson's name does figure briefly under the idealism of Concord in that most allusive of books. Stalling, I said that Emerson could not be the desired answer as I tried to fish among the hundreds of others in that ocean of unfamiliar names, and I felt more and more foolish as I cast again and again—John

Hay, Clarence King, *The Memoirs of Ulysses S. Grant*. I was just as likely to catch a *pteraspis* as the name of Darwin.

Miller's great skill as a teacher was exemplary rather than sympathetically imaginative. He had a brilliantly intuitive mind, an extraordinary ability to find the heart of a seventeenth-, eighteenth-, or nineteenth-century text. That gift, and the art of dramatizing intellectual history so that young students who had virtually no knowledge of theology would see both the passion and the intellectual complexity in the debates of narrow Puritans or corpse-cold Unitarians, made him a priceless teacher even though he apparently found it hard to imagine (as young people now say) where the student was coming from. He would talk down to us when he explained Calvinist predestination by reminding us that some of us who read all the assignments would win lower grades than an occasional carouser who had been granted the free gift of intellectual grace. He miscalculated the nature of my misinformation when he demonstrated the mildness of Emerson's iconoclasm by pointing out that Emerson's first vote as a member of the Harvard Board of Overseers was in favor of compulsory chapel. Perhaps through no fault of my high school teacher, I had come into Perry Miller's course with the conviction that transcendentalists had been a group of ineffective, ethereal yea-sayers, who saw beauty everywhere. For me and several of my friends, the great revelation in Miller's lectures on Emerson was his proof that in the 1830s Emerson was a dangerous man, a magnetic proponent of what Andrews Norton called the latest form of infidelity. When Miller intoned Emerson's stirring command to call a popgun a popgun even if the ancient and honorable of the earth affirm it to be the crack of doom, or Emerson's defiant "If I am the devil's child, let me speak as the devil's child," everyone in the lecture hall (Emerson D) must have felt the electricity. And when he traced his famous religious and philosophical line from Jonathan Edwards to Emerson, he made Emerson's remarks on the historicity of Jesus Christ's miracles sound like the crack of doom for the pale Unitarian negations against which Emerson was firing. Miller made me see why, in "that sublime jubilee of emotion," Emerson had said that "the very word Miracle, as pronounced by Christian churches . . . is Monster." And when Miller read Emerson's next clause from the address to the Harvard Divinity School —"It is not one with the blowing clover and the falling rain"—I wanted to cheer.

Although I suspect that the conservative wing of the Unitarian church did not receive perfectly fair treatment in Miller's memorable exposition, it was clear even then that he was not trying to recruit us into Emerson's camp. In showing us how subversively exciting Emerson's appeal had been, he showed us also how outrageously dangerous that appeal had seemed to established leaders in the Harvard Divinity School. Nor was Miller's magnetic lecturing technique, powerful though it was, his greatest asset. His husky voice, his imposing presence as he paced before a large audience or sat turning over his note cards before a smaller class, his energetic delivery of his own sometimes orotund pronouncements—all these helped to bring his lectures alive. I can still hear him declaiming in mock scorn his judgment of one of Van Wyck Brooks's most famous books: "And this explosion of resentment, this exasperated rejection of John Locke's sensationalism and Scottish Common Sense, this desperate epistemological quest in which young men—born, Emerson said, 'with knives in their brain'—were *driven* (Emerson also said) to find society, value, deity within themselves—this earthquake, this passionate revolution in religious, social, and literary thought, Mr. Van Wyck Brooks has deigned to call the *flowering* of New England!" But his chief exemplary value was not in the performance. For me the great point was his insistence on the complexity of human experience, the perplexity of historical human beings, the contradictory or at least paradoxical tension within systems of ideas.

He began the course in American romanticism, for example, by assigning a famous essay by Arthur O. Lovejoy, "On the Discrimination of Romanticisms." Only after we were all suitably chastened into avoiding the word *romanticism,* for fear of anti-historical shallowness, did we begin building with Perry Miller a conception of what romanticism had meant in the United States in the first half of the nineteenth century. At the first meeting of the class, Miller distributed an immense reading list, with an extraordinary number of titles—thirty-five, if I remember correctly—starred and therefore required reading during the twelve-week term. In each category the starred titles were followed by ten to fifteen others, and Miller told us at once that the thirty-five titles were "the barest *minimum*" with which some of the less industrious undergraduates might win their gentlemen's C's. All *serious* students, he said, would have to read most of the other titles as well, and of course he assumed that we all were well acquainted with the great works of Hawthorne and Melville. Here we would be concentrating on Hawthorne's *The Blithedale Romance* and Melville's *Pierre,* but those of us who had not yet read *The Scarlet Letter* and *Moby-Dick* would have to make up the deficiency in our own free time. The tone of all this bullying had a slight hint of mocking exaggeration that struck me and my closest friends as rather a challenge than a condescending display. It had something of the same psychological effect as the command that Miller issued to his graduate seminar when I enrolled in it three years later. There he forbade us to praise our fellow students' papers. "Let us be brutal," he said, "for we love one another." He was telling us that the road to the Heavenly City of scholarship demanded arduous labor, reading in extremely diverse and abundant materials, not only to test our dedication and endurance but to lead us through the living centers of historical experience. Occasionally he might condescend to one of the romantic conventions he was delineating, as he did when he spoke contemptuously of Mrs. Lydia Sigourney's poem on the baptism of an infant at its mother's funeral. But the lesson that he exemplified was unmistakably clear: When scholarship had identified a literary convention, the most valuable work had only begun. One had to try to understand how the convention functioned as a way of giving meaning to human experience. Rather than expose the convention as a mere cliché, one had to see how much meaning and what a range of value it enabled a writer to convey.

In lecturing on these nineteenth-century materials, as in writing the studies of seventeenth-century Puritanism that had made his reputation, Miller brought us into contact with highbrows, middlebrows, and lowbrows. Mrs. Sigourney's sentimental poems and John Stone's melodramatic play *Metamora* lived for us in the same historical world as Cooper's *The Pioneers,* Melville's *Pierre,* John C. Calhoun's abstract *Disquisition on Government,* Stowe's *Uncle Tom's Cabin,* and Emerson's *Representative Men*. Miller delighted in tracing the course of a philosophical argument, whether in Calhoun's *Disquisition* on the concurrent majority or Melville's satirical assault on Emerson. In a graduate course on transcendentalism, the term had almost ended before Miller arrived at Emerson's work, for he had spent weeks tracing the theological line from seventeenth-century Puritans to nineteenth-century Unitarians, and several other weeks listening to our reports on minor transcendentalists. He took even more pleasure in demonstrating the power of ideas. So passionate was the antipathy expressed by American romantic writers against John Locke's "sensational" psychology in the generation before the Civil War that in Miller's lectures Locke appeared as almost villainous, the source of all defenses for the legalistic "head" or intellect against the higher, spiritual claims of the heart.

One of the most interesting combinations of opposing attitudes in Miller's own mind can be inferred from the catholicity of his reading lists and his lectures. He was eloquent in defending what he called the life of the mind, the value of scholarship, the importance of treating outmoded historical ideas seriously, with respect for their own terms. Yet he also belonged to the culture whose neglect of those values made his defense of them necessary. He wanted to be heard in his own time, not only by specialists but by general readers. His lectures often related the past to the immediate present. In 1946, that summer of triumph for the Boston Red

Sox, he compared Cooper's Leatherstocking, the natural man, to Ted Williams, the great left fielder for the Red Sox. Miller tried (unsuccessfully, he said) to find a modern analogue for the adoration of Byron in nineteenth-century American letters and for the broad expression of grief here over Byron's death. "See whether the cry of lamentation has the same ring in 1946 as in 1824," he said: "'Byron is dead!' 'Gertrude Stein is dead!'" In Ernest Hemingway's death fifteen years later, he found that analogue. Hemingway had been a fellow warrior, fellow Chicagoan, fellow aspirant to the achievement of high art without alienation from the general reader. I treasure the memory of Perry Miller in his army officer's trench coat at the top of the broad steps in front of Widener Library, drawing himself to attention, clicking his heels, and breaking off a crisp military salute as his stoop-shouldered senior colleague Arthur M. Schlesinger, carrying a heavy briefcase, labored up the steps. Miller was not just a scholar; he was a man of the world.

Of course there was considerable justification for the relevance of this attitude to the period we were studying, and many of us admired both Miller's willingness to make the effort and the aptness of some of his comparisons. It was Emerson's "The American Scholar," after all, that had portrayed (for all of us to emulate) the ideal of Man Thinking and then acting in the world. Even in the seventeenth-century New England mind to which Miller and Morison had introduced us, ministers had been admonished to make their highest thought intelligible to the meanest capacities. Within a year or two after the Second World War, moreover, the "present-ist" attitude seemed to win the sanction of the history department, which appointed Arthur M. Schlesinger, Jr., to an associate professorship with tenure after his *The Age of Jackson* had drawn strong lines connecting the 1830s and 1840s to the age of Franklin D. Roosevelt. With the announcement of the Marshall Plan at my Harvard commencement in 1947, the Truman Doctrine drawing a line in the same year against Soviet expansion toward western Europe, and Henry Wallace's challenge to Truman's Cold

War presidency in the campaign of 1948, many of us were deeply engaged in the same debates that engrossed our favorite teachers. We heard that Miller and Matthiessen had fallen out over professorial commitment to the tutorial system, which Matthiessen passionately supported but Miller found too time-consuming, and we knew that they disagreed sharply over the best way to end the Cold War as well as over the degree to which the United States was responsible for the chill. I still remember the joy Miller expressed from the podium as we assembled for his lecture at noon on the day after Harry Truman's amazing victory in the election of 1948. With the Democratic vote split among the third-party Wallace Progressives and the fourth-party Thurmond Dixiecrats, Thomas Dewey had been sure to win, and we had all expected the necessary Republican votes to come rolling in during the hours before dawn. By noon it seemed clear that Truman had won. I do not remember that Miller said anything about the election in that lecture. As the scene plays in my memory, he waves his hand and mimes a shoulder-shaking laugh acknowledging congratulations and expressions of relief from some of the students, as if he himself had just been elected.

Yet our gratitude for this exemplary connection between the world of historical scholarship and the world of contemporary culture and politics was sometimes qualified by uneasiness. Hearing him twice a week over a period of several years, we became accustomed to his dramatic, even hyperbolic allusions. We learned to scale down his exaggerations in a way that outsiders, who met him only through his writings, might not discover. I was startled, though I should not even have been surprised, when Yvor Winters asked me one day soon after my arrival at Stanford, "Why doesn't Miller come clean on Calvinism?" Miller's discussion of the New England Puritans' Covenant of Grace had argued that emphasis on human claims under that covenant had amounted to a major departure from the Calvinist doctrine of predestination. I understood from long association with Miller that he believed the Puritans were at the same time Calvinists and modifiers of

Calvinism, and that his own technique had asked readers of *The New England Mind* to imagine a single national mind surviving through the seventeenth century despite his awareness that there had been no single version of Calvinism in New England. Had he heard Winters's query, Miller might have argued that "coming clean" begged the question, because the New England Puritans' version of Calvinism was a mixture of opposing tendencies. But Winters could have pointed to specific passages in which Miller had said that "the Puritans" were *not* Calvinists, and Donald Stanford, one of Winters's students, did point out not only that the poet Edward Taylor had been perfectly orthodox in preaching Calvinist doctrine, but also that Calvin himself had allowed, at least in preaching, for the kind of softening implicit in the Puritans' Covenant of Grace.

A similar argument developed over the so-called modernity of Jonathan Edwards. In his celebrated biographical study of Edwards's thought, Miller had stressed not only Edwards's brilliant use of Isaac Newton's physics and John Locke's psychology, but also Edwards's anticipation of modern issues in both physics and psychology. Edwards, he wrote, would have needed only "about an hour's reading in William James, and two hours in Freud, to catch up completely" on the relationship between reason and temperament. Miller's chief point, I believe, had been the presence of recognizably permanent issues, and an attempt to confront them honestly with the best scientific hypotheses of his time, in the thought of an eighteenth-century Calvinist whose name had become a byword of dogmatic terror. But the hyperbolic claim of modernity came at least partly from Miller's desire to win favor for the past, and for his own professional commitment, by showing it was like the very present whose provinciality he was otherwise rebuking.

Our affectionate admiration for his genius and his example did not blind us to these difficulties even when we were in his classes. Remembering his allusions to Ted Williams, some of us invented a baseball team made up of professors to whom we assigned the nicknames of major league stars. One of the pitchers was Harry (the Cat) Levin, whose quiet approach to literary prey and whose stress on the last syllable of his surname reminded us of the St. Louis Cardinals' quick-fielding southpaw, Harry (the Cat) Brecheen. The center fielder was F. O. Matthiessen, who rumor said had been too short to qualify for service as an officer in the army. We named him for Dominic DiMaggio of the Red Sox, who was known as the Little Professor. Sam (Boo) Morison we named for a Boston pitcher, Dave (Boo) Ferris; William Yandall Elliott, a blustering professor of government, for Bobo Newsom, a big, flamboyant pitcher. And Perry Miller we unanimously acclaimed as the winner of Ted Williams's title, the Kid.

Because of his dramatic energy, the broad range of his reading, and his seemingly voracious appetite for theology and philosophy as well as literature, Miller acquired a reputation as an exhaustive scholar as well as a perceptively creative interpreter of the past. I imagined him as Thomas Wolfe's hero ranging through the stacks of Widener. He declared with characteristic flourish that the bibliography for the first volume of *The New England Mind* consisted of everything published in New England in the seventeenth century. Some of his less reliable generalizations were therefore accepted as literally as if they had carried the authority of scientific fact. He was indeed a fine scholar, thoroughly dedicated to his work, and his most important interpretations of American history and literature have a firm base in his original research. On large and small subjects, however, he was capable not only of error but of roundly proclaiming as fact that which he had offered no evidence to support. I do not mean only the generalization that the seventeenth-century Puritans preached no hellfire sermons; finding a few powerful ones did shake my faith in his authority for a time, but I saw even then that a slight revision of the statement would probably suffice. Nor was the occasional lifting of a quotation out of context the main problem, although a critic who challenged the modernity of Jonathan Edwards displayed a few of those in his dispute with Miller. Every interpretative scholar is susceptible to that infirmity. What troubled me was the belated discovery that some of his statements which looked like mere statements of fact were actually wishful interpretations which were not true.

The most embarrassing of these for me was the statement in *The New England Mind: The Seventeenth Century* that Puritan preachers did not use rhetoric in the first two sections of the standard sermon, the sections in which the preacher stated doctrines and gave reasons to support their validity. Only after turning from Doctrines and Reasons to Uses (or the Application), Miller says, did the preacher use rhetoric, the metaphors, similes, tropes—"bait to catch the will and affections"—that were designed to bring the lesson home to the auditor's heart. I was already teaching early American literature, and had repeated this alleged truth to my Stanford undergraduates, before I learned that it was false. We learned together that it was false when we read some of the actual sermons that Miller had chosen to reprint in an anthology, for in Thomas Hooker's sermons we found striking figurative language early and late. Miller's idea had been splendid; he had wanted to tie the three subjects of grammar, logic, and rhetoric to the doctrines, reasons, and uses into which Puritan sermons had usually been divided, because the Puritans had mistrusted rhetoric as a potentially seductive power, which could be safely used only after the strictest rules of grammatical and logical analysis had been applied in the preacher's opening of a biblical text. At some point in his composition, perhaps, Miller had seen the elegance of the parallels, and had then remembered how strongly the rhetoric predominates in the sections of sermons called applications or uses. It seems plausible to me that his exposition of his insight then ran afoul of his dramatic power, so that either with a thought of checking the generalization before publishing the book, or else in the exhilaration of the moment, he simply declared that ministers did not use rhetoric in the first two sections of their sermons.

The error itself was minor. It is worth recording here only to illustrate an important point about Miller's exemplary role in

American literary and historical scholarship. His own powerful rhetoric, his broad reading, his bibliographical claims, and the relative obscurity of his seventeenth-century sources—all helped to establish his reputation as not only a gifted interpreter but also a meticulous and exhaustive scholarly witness. His brilliant use of a great variety of quotations gave his argument authority. Unless one went to Harvard, however, to examine a typescript Miller had deposited there, one could not follow that argument closely through the trails usually marked in footnotes, because he did not specifically annotate any of his major books.* As his reputation flourished in the 1950s and 1960s, and as the boom in American literary and historical scholarship led more young people to the seventeenth-century documents, some investigators were startled by the discrepancies they found. The assault upon portions of his work was therefore partly a result of his success in helping to stimulate further investigation of the period and in understating the degree to which his best work depended on insight or speculation rather than thorough accumulation. One scholar, George Selement, went so far as to test Miller's declaration that annotating the first volume of *The New England Mind* would mean "republish[ing] the complete bibliography of early New England, with various additions, not merely once but many times over." Selement's actual count revealed that Miller had cited only fifteen percent of the published materials and very few manuscripts, and that nearly 70 percent of his quotations in that book had come from the works of only six ministers.

When I say that Miller's pedagogical skill was exemplary, I mean to include his attitude and his technique as well as the quality of his perceptions. He was a challenging questioner in undergraduate tutorial sessions and a tough oral critic of papers in his graduate seminar, but in his seminar and in directing Ph.D. theses he

*In 1981 James Hoopes edited Miller's notes for the first volume. See *Sources for "The New England Mind: The Seventeenth Century"* (Williamsburg: Institute of Early American History and Culture, 1981).

treated the student as a scholar who was already independent. A very few critical queries in the margin, perhaps a few vertical lines and question marks, and a pithy comment at the end—these were the substance of his written instruction. He would gladly discuss questions we brought to him while doing our research, but he communicated an emphatic message: You are scholars; do your work; learn to write; be professionals; bring me and the public your results. At the first meeting of his seminar on Hawthorne and Melville, he proposed a number of topics for our term papers, scheduled an individual conference with each of the six students to confirm the respective assignments, and appointed each of us as the critic to open the discussion of a fellow student's paper. Then he adjourned the seminar until six weeks before the end of the term, whereupon we met at his house one evening a week to hear and debate one of the papers. Those sessions lasted for three intense hours. After hearing the paper read aloud during the first hour, each of the five students had to comment critically on it before the author was allowed to respond. Then Miller delivered his own judgment of all six, served us beer, and let the debate range freely—though of course he was always a vigorous participant—until it was time to evict us at eleven. We usually went down the street arguing on the way home.

In his personal relationship with students, Miller was similarly generous and aloof. On this subject I am probably not the most representative of witnesses, for the accident of his assignment as my tutor led him to adopt me as a virtual protégé. He was gruffly informal, insisting that my wife and I call him Perry, and he invited us to his house along with his senior colleagues and graduate students. He expressed a warm admiration for Pat and a generous solicitude for her and our infant son when she came down with viral pneumonia. He cheerfully nominated me for the teaching fellowship that enabled me to stay in graduate school, and for my first full-time job a few years later. But he had difficulty crossing the gulf between the high country of intellectual history and the marshlands in which we splashed through our daily lives.

There was an awkward condescension in his gestures toward intimacy. One night he telephoned me at ten o'clock to tell me that in fifteen minutes a man from Bennington College would telephone to offer me a job. Of course I cannot remember the exact words, but I am sure that the heavily imperative syntax and tone are accurately conveyed in this summary: "Now David, in fifteen minutes you will receive a telephone call from Mr. Franklin Ford. He will offer you a job at Bennington. Tomorrow morning you will come over to Cambridge to be interviewed by him, but that will be a mere formality. On Thursday you will take the train to North Adams, where you will be met by the secretary to the president. . . ." Although I was offered an interview rather than a job, this report was reasonably accurate. The trouble was a false note in the Olympian tone. He had struck a similar note two or three years earlier, upon learning from a colleague who interviewed me for the teaching fellowship that I had expressed admiration for my former English A instructor. "Now Harry Levin, he's 'A,' and Oscar Handlin is 'A,' and I think you may be 'A-minus,' but John Lydenberg is 'B,' and you must not cite him as a model." I still dissent from that judgment, and I believe it represents an attitude that Warner Berthoff once named "Harvard bloody-mindedness." I have met the same attitude both west and south of Cambridge.

Usually, however, the commanding, condescending note sounded when Miller volunteered a personal favor, and it was in response to one of those ungraceful offers that I not only made some lifelong friends but gained further insight into Miller's complex character. When he heard that I was going to France in 1956 as a Fulbright exchange professor at the University of Strasbourg, he told me that I must seek out a Dr. Stahl immediately after my arrival. Dr. Stahl, he said, was an eminent medical professor who had been a hero of the French Resistance, and he would surely open doors for Pat and me. We had no intention of imposing ourselves upon Dr. Stahl, but after we had been in Strasbourg for six weeks the tenant in the flat below ours asked me whether it was possible that in so large a country as the United States I might happen to be acquainted with a Professor Perry Miller. She was a close friend of Dr. Stahl's secretary, who promptly arranged a feast worthy of a reunion with the returning American hero himself. Dr. Stahl was there, and each of us signed a post card to Perry Miller that began with "Dear Spy." Thereby hung the amusing tale.

Our hostesses, Sizy and Marthe Bischoff, had remained in Strasbourg throughout the war and Dr. Stahl had indeed been a leader of the Resistance there. Shortly before the Liberation, the flat in which we were now assembled had been exposed to view from the street when an American bomb had stripped a side wall off the building. Yet the devastation wrought by American B-24s (the Liberators) had not embittered these women against American soldiers. In the euphoria of the Liberation, the Bischoff sisters had gone to the university one afternoon to celebrate the opening of the first course in English (a subject forbidden during the German occupation), and there they had been accosted by a tall, helmeted American major, puzzling over a guide book, who had asked them how to find the Faculty of Letters. They told me that they had invited Professor/Major Perry Miller back to their apartment and had summoned Dr. Stahl to a dinner in honor of the liberator. Twelve years after the event, they laughed as they described what they took to be Miller's wary symbolism, the ostentatious removal of his .45-caliber pistol and cartridge belt, which he deposited carefully on a table in the foyer. They too had disarmed themselves, they said, for they had not only brought out wines and delicacies saved for such an occasion but had answered his eager questions with confidential stories about the Resistance.

With warm declarations of friendship, then, and promises to return one day, the major had taken up his pistol and had disappeared. A German counteroffensive had begun the next day, and Leclerc's army, to which Miller was attached, had left Strasbourg. For weeks thereafter the Bischoff sisters and Dr. Stahl had regretted their indiscreet revelations to this stranger, and for years they had interpreted his silence as evidence that he had really been a

German spy. In 1948 or 1949, while a visiting professor at the University of Leiden, Miller had arranged to lecture at the University of Strasbourg, and he had written in advance to explain his long silence and to propose a grand reunion with the Bischoffs and Dr. Stahl. Our first meeting with them in 1956 reenacted that reunion, and for a quarter of a century now we have kept in touch with the Bischoffs. In the summer of 1980 we visited them again for an hour late one morning; I thought affectionately of Perry Miller not only when we all reviewed the story of the spy but also when the sisters expressed surprise at my reluctance to drink whiskey, as my mentor had done, at eleven o'clock in the morning.

"Why," my mother asked me when she met Miller at last in 1960, "does a man with such a fine mind want to destroy himself?" She had expected my eminent mentor to exude sober wisdom, but he had obviously been drinking heavily before he arrived to dine with us in the house we were renting in Cambridge that summer. His doctors had warned him several years earlier that alcohol gravely threatened his life, and three years after my mother asked her unanswerable question alcohol surely did contribute to his death (from acute pancreatitis) at the age of fifty-eight. I could not forget that F. O. Matthiessen had committed suicide at forty-eight. Whether Miller's drinking, in the last five years of his life, was reckless or actually suicidal, the second of our two most influential teachers of American literature had destroyed himself when—as the survival of Morison, Schlesinger, Frederick Merk, and Howard Mumford Jones eventually showed—decades of productive scholarship might have been available to him. I cannot explain the mystery of self-destruction any more than the marvel of creativity. Yet an essay on exemplary qualities must try to take some account of their relationship to unhealthy traits in the same character.

Our frivolity was not completely aimless when we listed Miller on our professorial baseball team as the Kid. For all his intellectual distinction, there was a boyishness about him that seemed to plead for one's protective understanding. I do not mean that he would ever have applied to himself the quotation that he loved to cite from Cooper's Natty Bumppo, "I am a plain unlarned man." No, he wanted to live in the world of learning on terms that respected all the disciplines contributing to intellectual history. One of his finest qualities as a teacher was the gusto with which he spoke the language of theology, philosophy—even physics—as if we were all engaged on equal terms in a colloquy with the most distinguished citizens in the republic of letters. He was our senator in that republic, our priest in the temple of learning. But naturally, then, there was an ingenuously thespian quality about him, as if he embodied the intellectual issues. He liked nothing better than presenting ideas and tendencies as a dialectic and describing heroic efforts to reconcile them—in the Puritans, in Jonathan Edwards, in R. W. Emerson, and Reinhold Niebuhr. Not only in explicating them but in his own life, Miller himself seemed to express the hunger to achieve and to reconcile that he described so movingly in historical figures and in the Byronic hero. In his late forties, he himself seemed to resemble the young Byron more than old Captain Ahab. The scholar and the creative artist, the scholar and the man of the world, the scholar and the hearty democrat, the historian and the original philosopher influencing his own time—I imagine that perceiving the discrepancy between even *his* prodigious reach and his actual grasp cost Miller heavily. I cannot say why a mind that penetrated so acutely as his into historical failures of a similar kind failed to check its own impulses toward attempting the impossible, or failed to see them more humorously. Perhaps it was those impulses that led him to see so acutely into the historical failures. I am left with the image that Miller himself described in one of his few autobiographical essays: the sixteen-year-old Chicagoan who had run off from home to ship out on the crew of a freighter sits among barrels of case oil in an African port and, in a vision like Gibbon's near the ruins on the Capitoline Hill, decides to write the intellectual history of his country. For what he taught me about that history through his writing and about the scholarly life through his example as a teacher, I salute him gratefully.

F. O. Matthiessen

Everyone I knew called him Matty. Before the war he served as chairman of the interdepartmental Committee on Undergraduate Degrees in History and Literature, and I met him briefly in November 1942 when I belatedly applied for admission to the program. His baldness called attention to his tapered crown, and his rimless glasses often reflected light from the thick top of the lenses because, short though he was, he habitually looked downward toward the desk or, as he spoke brusquely for emphasis, moved only his eyes rather than lift his head when he looked directly at his interlocutor. His speech in both conversation and lectures was often brisk, with marked pauses between phrases, and his characteristic gesture for emphasis used both forearms, one a few inches above the other, in a sharp, downward, slicing motion. Even in our first interview his manner seemed to combine authority with the vulnerability that made young students who had never spoken to him refer to this diminutive scholar by using the diminutive form of his surname. Whether or not we believed the rumor that he had been rejected as a volunteer for military service because he was not tall enough, everyone could recognize a nervous shyness about him which qualified his brusqueness, and a friendliness which removed most of the awesomeness from his achievement as a critic and scholar.

I had not read a line of Matthiessen's published work, but I knew before our first interview that he might function for me as a reconciler. His reputation had given me the welcome word. I did not know what a New Critic was, only that Matthiessen had written a book called *The Achievement of T. S. Eliot,* that he advocated literary criticism as well as scholarship in the university, and that he defended the teaching of both American literature and modern poetry. My roommate told me, moreover, that Matthiessen had just recently published a masterpiece called *American Renaissance,* which combined close literary criticism with social and cultural analysis.

Matthiessen and his program in history and literature appeared to me as reconciler and refuge, respectively, because I had been struggling with advice from three less illustrious elders who had taken an interest in my education. In the oversimplified conflict that my memory now depicts, two of my favorite high school teachers stand in an improbable alliance against my freshman-English instructor at Harvard, John Lydenberg.

Dolly Gulden stands as a silent member of the alliance. It was for her fourth-year Latin class that I had translated the first book of the *Aeneid* into heroic couplets, and she had urged me to show this alliterative marvel to my teachers at Harvard. John Lydenberg's comments and grades on my first overwritten themes had dissuaded me from taking her advice, but even as I began reading more eagerly in contemporary literature I felt loyally committed to Miss Gulden's belief that the first requirement of a liberal education demands knowledge of the great literary tradition.

The very terms in which Harvard had first been called to my attention had emphasized a tradition of learning rather than any studies of contemporary life. It was John Rouse, my high-school tennis coach, who had protested when he learned that I was about to apply for admission to Ursinus College. He simply insisted that I go to a university which had a great library. He had graduated from Harvard in 1933, and he told me that in Widener Library I could find any book I wanted. To illustrate this wonder, he did not describe Eugene Gant or Thomas Wolfe roaming the stacks and devouring books. I am sure that John Rouse had not read Wolfe, for he would have closed *Look Homeward, Angel* before reaching the second page. No, his illustration for me offered access to the recondite. If I wandered into the stacks in search of a book by George Psalmanazar, Rouse assured me, it would be there, among books by the great and the obscure. I remembered the name of Psalmanazar from the opening lines of Jonathan Swift's "A Modest Proposal," but of course I knew nothing about the prodigious impostor, who for a time had persuaded all London that he was a Formosan convert to Christianity.

John Rouse made it clear during this first discussion that one should go to Harvard to read Samuel Johnson and Jonathan Swift rather than George Psalmanazar, but the accessibility of great stores of learning was almost as important to him as the ideological significance of his reverence for Dr. Johnson. Even at fifteen and sixteen, I had been able to see at least some of that political meaning when he questioned my hearty approval of Franklin D. Roosevelt, Sinclair Lewis, and Richard Wright, and when he tried to cool my fiery reaction to news of German successes in the war. I had simply assumed, grateful though I surely was, that I was entitled to the innumerable hours of serious attention he gave me and that at least part of his resistance to my hawkish fulminations grew out of a prudent concern for my safety. (He thought I might run off and join the navy on my seventeenth birthday, in the middle of my first term at Harvard, and a year later he disapproved of my enlistment in the army air force.) Without having changed my political and social views, then, I had gone to Harvard to learn about the past. I had promptly confirmed John Rouse's promise that a freshman could find George Psalmanazar's work in the stacks of Widener and had astonished my instructor in "English Literature from Beowulf to Yeats" by writing a paper on Psalmanazar.

John Lydenberg's role in this little drama was to stand in politics and literature for the present. He had actually assigned a fair number of nineteenth-century masterpieces—*Adventures of Huckleberry Finn,* for example, and *The Brothers Karamazov*—but for me the liberating message of his course was contemporary and political.

The Autobiography of Lincoln Steffens introduced me to the pervasiveness of graft and the complexity of reform; Thomas Mann's "Mario and the Magician," to the psychological and moral horrors of totalitarianism. We read stories by Erskine Caldwell and novels by Ernest Hemingway, John Dos Passos, and F. Scott Fitzgerald. For my term paper, due in May as the culminating work of the entire academic year, I chose to write about the novels and criticism of James T. Farrell, whose trilogy *Studs Lonigan* had won popular and critical acclaim for grim descriptions of Irish-American life in Chicago. I also decided that anyone who wanted to be a writer in the mid-twentieth century ought to know as much as possible about government and politics. I chose government as my field of concentration.

John Rouse deplored virtually all these developments. His congratulations on the prize awarded to my essay about Farrell did not inhibit him from warning that Farrell was simply unworthy of my time. Farrell's "tin-eared realism" and Erskine Caldwell's gruesome stories would soon drop into the swamps; Shakespeare and Samuel Johnson would always shine. The marvel to me now is that I seem never to have doubted whether my two generous friends and teachers had anything better to do with their own time than debate the merits of my curricular decisions. Each of them taught me much by challenging my assumptions and interpreting individual books. (Although I never had a course with Rouse, his questions about my extracurricular reading and about the prose in my sports columns for the *York High Weekly* were no less acute than his analyses of tennis strokes and strategy.) My instructed memory honors them both for giving a confused, self-preoccupied young student the precious gift of time. For a week or two in the autumn of 1942, I even had the two of them tied up in an indirect epistolary debate—their letters traveling from York or Bennington College, where Lydenberg had accepted a full-time appointment, to the respective antagonist by way of my room in Lowell House.

A few weeks before joining the army, then, I found in Matthiessen's example and in his program a hope of reconciling the two kinds of conflicting tendencies that had been worrying me. History and literature would enable me to return to the study of literature and yet to continue studying what I took to be social and political change; and the new program, with Matthiessen's example, would encourage attention to both literary history and contemporary writers. I stayed in college long enough to complete the abbreviated semester, long enough to confirm (with the help of a generous tutor, Bernard Bowron) the soundness of my choice.

When I returned to Harvard three years later, Matthiessen still chaired the program in history and literature. My years in the Middle West, South, and Southwest, living in barracks with a much greater variety of fellow citizens than I could otherwise have met, had intensified my curiosity about American culture. Surely my personal reasons for that commitment could be matched with counterparts in the individual lives of my classmates, but some more general circumstances (along with the exhilaration and the eminent exemplars I have already described) must help to explain the unusually large number who made similar choices. In my Harvard College class of 1945 alone, Robert Cross, Justin Kaplan,* Kenneth Lynn, Charles Sellers, John William Ward, and I all went on to write books about American history and literature; Warner Berthoff, class of 1947, studied and graduated with us. Proof that Berthoff's name belongs on the same list is Leo Marx's decision to recommend Berthoff, Cross, and me for admission to graduate school in a single letter. I still don't know whether that letter accounts for Kenneth Murdock's repeated confusion of Levin and Berthoff throughout our graduate years. I can only report that twenty years later, while on leave at Harvard for a year, I gave Murdock an inscribed offprint of an article; several days later he met

*Kaplan concentrated in English rather than history and literature, and he graduated during the war, because he was physically ineligible for military service. But of course his biographies of Mark Twain, Steffens, and Whitman stand alongside other achievements in American studies of the last half-century.

Berthoff in the library and congratulated him for having written my article.

In 1946, then, I came to know Matthiessen as the scholar who presided over an extraordinarily harmonious and yet diverse community. Political scientists, classicists, literary critics, and historians of everything from economics and religion to art and architecture—professors, teaching fellows, and a few undergraduates (no more than fifty, as I recall, entering in any one year)—concentrated individually and in small groups on a nation's history and literature (Germany, France, England, the United States), or the history and literature of four countries in one traditional period, or of Greece or Rome. One adventurous student even chose the history and literature of Greece and India. Arthur M. Schlesinger, Jr.'s prodigious undergraduate honors thesis, a biography of Orestes A. Brownson, had been published before the war; now Schlesinger had joined the faculty as associate professor of history, and everyone was talking about his new book, *The Age of Jackson*. Oscar Handlin was broadening our definition of social history with his lectures (sponsored by the Committee on Social Relations?) on immigration. Louis Hartz was volubly defending in government the interpretation that would lead to his courses and his book on the liberal tradition in American politics. In that heady time just after the war, American studies had a special élan, in which I was perfectly happy to immerse myself as uncritically as anyone. But we all knew that the program in history and literature was much broader than the American section that had a disproportionately large population, and any doubts about provinciality were at least partly allayed by the requirement that every student pass an examination on an ancient author and an ancient historian (Sophocles and Thucydides), as well as another on the Bible and Shakespeare. In alternate years, moreover, our leader, F. O. Matthiessen, replaced his friend Theodore Spencer as professor in the standard, year-long course on Shakespeare. If Matthiessen created a hyperbole in the title *American Renaissance* (which one of my learned classmates called an oxymoron), he did not pay mere lip service to the original Renaissance. His comparison grew out of scholarly knowledge of both seventeenth-century English literature and the special affection that Emerson, Melville, and Hawthorne felt for Shakespeare, Montaigne, Spenser, Milton.

Although it was not primarily as a teacher that I knew Matthiessen, he did exemplify in the classroom some qualities which became important to me when I decided to enter the profession. Surely there must be some craft or art, something of the performer, in any public presentation of self, but of all the distinguished lecturers I heard at Harvard in those years none gave so clearly as Matthiessen the impression that he was *not* giving a performance, that he was speaking directly to each student in the room. Other styles had their own value. Perry Miller's oratorical splendor, as he turned over note cards, often had a dramatic impact, especially when the intellectual issues and the historical personality allowed him to emphasize paradox or conflict. Arthur M. Schlesinger, Sr., was wise to read his lectures from a typewritten text, because they contained too much information to be entrusted to a combination of notes and extemporaneous sentences. The trouble was that one small but significant portion of his notorious examinations required us to identify minute facts from those lectures—the inventor of the twine binder or the barbed-wire fence; I was so busy recording the name of Mrs. Hannah Montague Lord of Troy, New York as inventor of the detachable collar, and recording a thousand other facts as well as Schlesinger's innovative questions about social and intellectual history, that I had no time to listen seriously to what he was saying. His insights into social history had led an entire generation of specialists to study new kinds of questions, and even in his sixties his original comments on large issues sank in *after* I had gone home to review my notes at the end of the day. I did look up now and then during the lecture to see him twisting his forelock with a pencil as he read, or marking his text (was he recording the intensity of the laughter?) just after he had read one of the epigrams, jokes, or puns that were scattered through his lectures: Paul Revere was a highly skilled silversmith and the father of fifteen children—which indicates that he did not spend all his time on horseback; the war between religion and geology was a battle between the Rock of Ages and the Age of Rocks; if mankind does not end war, war will end mankind; the free-waist movement was gaining sway, but the iron-bound corset still held its own. In contrast to Miller, Schlesinger, and several others, Matthiessen seemed in his hesitant speech to be enlisting us in his search for the right words, and then to speak those words *to* us as if his whole being stood behind them and as if he cared intensely whether each of us received the message.

He also showed that he wanted to hear our responses. Fifty or sixty students overflowed the steaming classroom in Sever Hall, a room adequate for perhaps thirty-five, at the first meeting of his course in twentieth-century American poetry, in the summer of 1946. Matthiessen entered, draped his seersucker jacket over a chair, and said, "I come from California, where one wears a coat to keep warm." Then he invited us to interrupt his lectures with questions or dissent, and he established a system of reports by graduate students to open the class meetings once or twice a week. The balding veteran in army trousers who gave the first of those reports (a critique of E. A. Robinson's poems) read it in rhyming couplets. I was intimidated by the display, although we undergraduates were not involved in the implicit competition, and I continued to resent the memory of that performance until, ten years later, when I had already been settled for some time at Stanford, I befriended James Kerans, the balding rhymer himself, who had recently joined the Stanford faculty. He told me that at the time of his performance he had been neither a graduate student nor even an upperclassman, but a lowly freshman. In appealing Matthiessen's refusal to admit him to the course, Kerans had volunteered to demonstrate his competence by giving the first oral report of the term. Ten years after the command performance, he insisted that he had not really been qualified to enroll, but we agreed that Matthiessen's response to him, though intimidating, had exemplified the classroom's openness to fresh air throughout the hot summer. Not only Dr. Leslie Fiedler, an auditor who challenged Matthiessen more than once from the floor, but any student—even the precocious freshman—was welcome to respond when Matthiessen opened one discussion of Ezra Pound (for example) by asking whether it is possible to write a good anti-Semitic poem.

Except for a generalized sense of what I would have called his democratic values, I was unaware of Matthiessen's political opinions until the Truman Doctrine became a major issue in the spring of 1947. Leo Marx, who had succeeded Perry Miller as my tutor and had helped me immeasurably in constructing and revising an honors thesis, deplored President Harry Truman's threat of intervention to prevent a Communist victory in Greece. (That way of defining the conflict was Truman's, of course, and not Leo Marx's or Matthiessen's.) It was through Leo Marx that I learned of Matthiessen's alarm over the Cold War. Our discussions continued beyond my first Harvard commencement exercises. I attended the morning ceremony, but missed hearing George C. Marshall's stirring proposal, in his speech to the Harvard alumni that afternoon, of massive expenditures to rehabilitate western Europe.

(My family missed the historic speech because in those days women were still excluded from the alumni spread, the luncheon served in the Yard on Commencement Day. Pat and I had invited Benjamin and Mildred Cohen, my prewar roommate's parents, to lunch in our apartment in Brighton. While the secretary of state was describing the Marshall Plan, my father and Mr. Cohen were agreeing that their sons the aerial navigators had been extremely fortunate to survive because, in Mr. Cohen's memorable words, "man was not born to fly.")

Matthiessen's objection to the Marshall Plan was the opposite of Senator Robert Taft's. On the six-o'clock news we heard Taft say, in response to an interviewer, "I haven't read the whole proposal, but off-hand I'd say we ought to cut it in half." Leo Marx explained to me that Matthiessen wanted the plan extended to the devastated socialist and Communist countries as well, and to Czechoslovakia. Marshall had indeed included the USSR and its satellites in the original offer, and a number of the Eastern European governments wanted to participate in the conference to work out the details of cooperation. Many people in both East and West, however, saw the plan as an effort to save the governments in western Europe from falling under Communist control after a winter that had exacerbated the miseries of the long war. Stalin and the eastern countries refused to participate in the conference, and Matthiessen attributed that decision at least partly to the anti-Communist rhetoric and actions of our own government. The only hope of avoiding the ultimate catastrophe, Matthiessen believed, lay in refusing to provoke or accept a split between the superpowers (though I believe that term was coined after his death). When he went to Austria that summer to inaugurate the Salzburg Seminar in American Civilization, and then to Prague for a term as visiting professor at Charles University, he welcomed students and colleagues from Left and Right. He reported on his return to Harvard that he had been denounced by both radical and conservative newspapers in Prague, and in his new book, *From the Heart of Europe,* he portrayed Czechoslovakia as a democratic society that could accommodate large Communist factions as well as a variety of liberal and conservative groups. He envisioned a socialist democracy that was not totalitarian, that knew how to live in the world of Josef Stalin without adopting his methods. Surely the Stalinist coup and the imprisonment and subsequent murder or suicide of Jan Masaryk, the man who embodied Matthiessen's hopes for an open society, grieved Matthiessen as sorely as any observer or visitor. Yet *From the Heart of Europe,* with its plea for generous trust between East and West, was excoriated in the press and in Cambridge as if its naïf author had invited Stalin's tanks to invade Prague.

My own uncertain judgment in these large matters had come down on the side of Truman and Marshall, but most of my political attention in the summer of 1947 had been focused on Boston's mayor, James Michael Curley, convicted of fraudulent use of the mails and imprisoned in the federal penitentiary at Danbury, Connecticut. Curley's last official act before going to Danbury had certified my appointment and dozens of others as playground instructors for the summer. I was assigned to Franklin Park, surrounded by the largely Jewish neighborhoods of Roxbury and Dorchester. An old reformer named Joseph Lee was the commissioner or city councilman who greeted us all at the one day of general introduction to the Park Department's rules and procedures. I was astonished to hear Mr. Lee ask us all to give a daily, grateful thought to Mayor Curley, whose personal troubles had not shut his eyes to the needs of Boston's children. Despite my reading of Lincoln Steffens, I had continued to think of Curley as simply a corrupt politician. Throughout that delightful, dusty summer, as I coached two boys' baseball teams, supervised the morning activities in Franklin Park, and played several baseball games a week, my thoughts hardly ever approached nearer to Matthiessen, political morality, and the Salzburg Seminar than Mayor Curley's cell in Danbury. There the mayor continued to issue at least some orders to his administration in Boston. I thought the supply of baseballs, bats, and catchers' equipment too mean for a daily population of more than seven hundred children, but I learned that until Curley intervened personally (with the concurrence of Lee) there had been no equipment at all. My team of sixteen-year-olds had only one baseball and no uniforms, but they had regulation bases and a regular schedule. Two or three evenings a week, moreover, I loved staying at the park to see the fields fill up with men who came to play in softball leagues, and even a series of cricket matches. The good things about the playground, including the affectionate loyalty the full-time staff expressed for Curley, sent me back to Steffens's portrayal of Martin Lomasny, the Boston boss who got things done and, though certainly no civic paragon, kept his political word. I was not surprised when the Republican legislature voted unanimously to pay Curley his mayoral salary while he remained in jail.

In the intervening decades I have often remembered that while Matthiessen was working out his hopeful interpretation of political complexity in Czechoslovakia I was trying to find reason for hope in urban politics. It was after his return from Czechoslovakia that I came to know him well enough to dare writing this memoir. The two years remaining in his life must have been increasingly miserable for him as he watched the Cold War grow more dangerously hostile, the search for "un-American activities" expand into McCarthyism, the laments for Czechoslovakia include attacks upon his book and his character. In the presidential election of 1948, Matthiessen supported Henry Wallace's Progressive party in what seemed to him a final opportunity to repudiate the Cold War. He gave a nominating speech for Wallace at the convention—surely the only political speech (said one of my friends) in which the speaker himself, without the aid of a hired writer, quoted both Walt Whitman and William James. Matthiessen thus angered many of his liberal colleagues, who thought either that Wallace and Matthiessen were "soft on communism" or at least that Wallace's campaign and the segregationists' new Dixiecrat (States' Rights) party would ensure a Republican victory and an intensified witch hunt against former radicals and Communists.

I knew nothing about the grief in Matthiessen's personal life that would exacerbate these public inflictions of pain, but fellow students did report that the celebrated discussions in his classes tended more often now to become political, and his remarks increasingly harsh. All the more remarkable, then, was Matthiessen's friendly participation in the organization in which I came to know him a little better, the Harvard Teachers' Union, an affiliate of the American Federation of Labor. I joined the union at the beginning of my teaching fellowship, in the autumn of 1948, as a gesture of collegiality. No great issues divided the union and the Harvard administration; I was simply persuaded that anyone who stood to benefit from the union's activities ought to support it and participate in its decisions. The great issue in those first months, the national presidential campaign, concerned the union only indirectly. So few of us turned up at the luncheon meetings and there was so little official business that our informal discussions soon revealed our preferences in the campaign. I came out for Truman, but I never heard a harsh word from Matthiessen on that subject or any other.

More remarkable than Matthiessen's forbearance in a time of increasing strain was his loyal participation in the union at a time when it was virtually moribund. Many distinguished people still belonged and paid their dues; when I became treasurer two or three years later, I collected checks from Harry Levin and Perry Miller. But Harlow Shapley and F. O. Matthiessen were the only eminent professors who still attended meetings and occasionally accepted election to office. The union, I learned, had flourished in the 1930s. Its crisis had come in the fierce debates over the Hitler-Stalin pact of 1939 and then over American neutrality or "isolation" in the first year of World War II. Scores of faculty members had joined in those debates, and the bitter division had split the union. Some of the hostility from those old battles persisted and flared up in new contempt during the late 1940s, but most professors, whether members or not, simply ignored the union.

What impressed me most memorably in Matthiessen, then, was the intensity of his conscientious citizenship. I saw it most clearly in the union, when I had already grown accustomed to his curricular responsibility. In the very years of his subjection to the pressures I have already sketched, this apparently lonely man, whose shyness or awkwardness seemed to make social activity unusually difficult for him, defended the tutorial system, wrote *From the Heart of Europe,* edited the historical anthology *The James Family,* coedited *The Notebooks of Henry James,* wrote *Theodore Dreiser* (published posthumously), worked vigorously in the presidential campaign, and served for a time not only as the Harvard Teachers' Union's president but then as its delegate to the AFL's Central Labor Union. (Perry Miller, who as a boy had shipped out on a freighter to Africa, had also served as the delegate before I was eligible to join.)

My classmate Warner Berthoff, who succeeded Matthiessen as the delegate to meet with representatives from all the other local affiliates of AFL, told me that Matthiessen had warned him not to expect an easy acceptance among the workers. I suppose Matthiessen's experience had resembled that of Hawthorne's narrator in *The Blithedale Romance,* who observes when the hired farmer is invited to dine with the sophisticated reformers that it is easier to condescend than to be condescended to. I find it hard to imagine Matthiessen's monthly meetings with the teamster, the carpenter, and the plumber, but his collegiality and his egalitarianism were so conscientiously pervasive that I never felt condescended to when he met with a handful of teaching fellows, junior colleagues, and one or two professors at the monthly meetings of our local chapter.

Matthiessen's egalitarianism had a social significance that now strikes me as comparable to the reactions of other aristocratic families with whom those years put me in touch. I knew that Matthiessen had graduated from Yale, but it was only when he collided with Henry Luce, the founder and publisher of *Time,* that I learned of Matthiessen's social standing. An article in *Time* described Matthiessen as a Marxist or a Communist. He wrote a letter to the editor, insisting that he was not a Marxist but a Christian and a socialist (he rejected the title Christian socialist), a communicant of the Episcopal church. Henry Luce then telephoned Matthiessen and invited him to lunch during Luce's next visit to Boston.

Reports of that private luncheon said not only that the reunion had been amicable, but that both Luce and Matthiessen belonged to Skull and Bones, a secret society at Yale whose members are supposedly obliged to leave the room whenever an outsider mentions the society's name. One of many folk tales about our eminent teachers portrayed Matthiessen as having somehow left his Skull and Bones pin at the home of his friend, colleague, and Beacon Hill neighbor Kenneth Murdock. Without explaining how such a pin could have been left at the home of a friend who was not a member, the story represents Matthiessen as telephoning Murdock without explicitly mentioning the pin: "Kenneth, I'm afraid I left something at your house last night." And Murdock replies, "Yes, it *is* here, Matty; just walk in, and you'll find it on the table in the foyer."

When I first heard these stories about Luce's luncheon and the pin, I was delighted by the apparent eccentricity. My friends and I found something charming in our exemplary democrat's loyalty to so exclusive a secret society. Overlooking the uglier significance of restrictive memberships, we not only remembered that a black halfback named Levi Jackson was reputed to have been tapped for admission to Skull and Bones in our own day; we enjoyed noticing that our admirer of Walt Whitman and Theodore Dreiser was willing to be friendly with the likes of Henry Luce. Later we were glad to see that the dust jacket and frontispiece of Matthiessen's *Theodore Dreiser* flaunted one of Matthiessen's favorite photographs: Dreiser in his socks. Sprawled in a chair, the shoeless figure who invites readers into Matthiessen's last book reminds one of the loafer whose relaxed image greets the reader of *Leaves of Grass*. And in his last lecture on *An American Tragedy* Matthiessen concluded with a moving line that named his bond with Dreiser: "I'm just a small-town boy myself."

A more somber report about Matthiessen's pin could be verified by anyone willing to look up the police records: among the personal belongings left on a table beside the suicide notes in his hotel room in 1950, police found Matthiessen's Skull and Bones pin. Thirty-seven years later that pin tells me little more than it did when I first heard about it. I admired Matthiessen as a man who might easily have joined Luce and T. S. Eliot in espousing right-wing political causes, just as he could have abandoned the tutorial system or the teachers' union and joined those colleagues who had decided to concentrate almost exclusively on their scholarship; just as he could have joined some of his neighbors by opening his home in Louisbourg Square to outsiders only on Christmas Eve and excluding those lesser folk from his life during the year. The intensity of his concern for undergraduate instruction, civil liberties, collegiality in the faculty, peace in the world, and democracy in the political economy—that intensity of commitment seemed to me the more admirable after I had learned of the small-town boy's patrician connections.

In my ignorance, the two chief lessons that I learned from this extraordinary teacher's example were the value of the qualities I have tried to describe here and the inadequacy of our sketches of our own teachers and colleagues. It was in Matthiessen's class that I had first read E. A. Robinson's *Eros Turannos,* in which the poet comments on his narrative of a wretched marriage,

> We tell you, tapping on our brows,
> The story as it should be,—
> As if the story of a house
> Were told, or ever could be;

but it was not until after Matthiessen's suicide (April 1, 1950) that I perceived the inadequacy of my terminology for his own life, and not until more than three decades later that some of the most enlightening information happened to come to me.

Of my reaction to Matthiessen's death, I remember my grief better than any sense of betrayal or desertion. Even then I understood that suicide probably cannot be explained by political anxiety or disappointment. But although Matthiessen explicitly told his friends that he could not know how large a part his concern about "the world situation" played in his decision, I came to regard him as a casualty of the Cold War and what later became known as McCarthyism. Matthiessen had seemed exhausted when I saw him for the last time, at a small reception in Laurence Holland's room in Winthrop House, in March 1950. I remember noticing that he had to reach his elbow up a little to lean on the mantle as he spoke to me, and that his face looked thin, his eyelids dark. He told me he had just finished a draft of his book on Dreiser, and that he felt worn out. I assumed that overwork had intensified his distress over the Cold War and his recent notoriety as the target of political scorn. I knew, too, that the sudden death of his friend Theodore Spencer had grieved him, but neither my closest friends nor I knew anything about Matthiessen's loneliness after the death of Russell Cheney several years earlier, nor about their domestic relationship, until Matthiessen's letters to Cheney were published a few years ago. The motives and anguish that impelled Matthiessen to jump from a hotel window must have been immeasurably more intricate than the political despair that I attributed to him. I see now that what moved him to his collegial egalitarianism must have been similarly complex, just as the Harvard Teachers' Union had a history considerably more complex than I then knew it to be.

When Matthiessen's letters to Russell Cheney were published, J. C. Levenson, who had known Matthiessen much better than I had known him, told me he was no less surprised than I at the revelation of the twenty-year "marriage" to Cheney, which had ended only with Cheney's death. Levenson *had* known, however, much more than I could have imagined about the significance of Matthiessen's continuing loyalty to Skull and Bones. As a guest in Matthiessen's summer home in Kittery, Maine, Levenson had seen Matthiessen in the role of godfather to a child from the Yale connection. And in a restaurant in Salzburg in 1947 he had heard Matthiessen's emphatic answer to a young colleague who asked, as naïvely as many of us might then have asked, why Matthiessen had never married. "I don't know," Matthiessen replied, "but one reason may be that my father and two brothers had nine wives among them."

I was surprised to learn recently that Matthiessen had once actually talked to Levenson about Skull and Bones: "They're my family. The first family I ever had." Until I read some of the letters to Russell Cheney, I had not been able to imagine the young Matthiessen's loneliness. Nor did I begin to comprehend, until I heard about his father, his brothers, and the first family he ever had, the depth of his loyalty to the few classmates who had been initiated into the secret society with him. I had been told that several of the honorary pallbearers at Matthiessen's funeral were members of Skull and Bones, whereas those who actually bore the weight included my friends Marx, Levenson, and Bowron; and I still remember the incongruous appearance of those two disparate groups in the crowded Christ Church on Concord Avenue. Only recently did I learn that the incongruous groups met harmoniously after the funeral in affectionate tribute to their mutual friend.

Levenson tells me that one of the suicide notes was addressed to him. Matthiessen asked forgiveness for the pain his death would cause, but he explained that he could not bear to re-experience the cycle of depression in which he had been caught. It was here that Matthiessen said he himself was unable to tell how much the world situation had to do with his depression. I begin to see now that, real though they surely were, the political and personal miseries about which I knew a little in the last year of Matthiessen's life reflected deeper problems, and more intense efforts to solve them, than I had considered even in my most tentative suppositions.

Two years after Matthiessen's death, as the brief heyday of McCarthyism approached the shameful moment when the Republican presidential nominee would campaign beside Senator Joseph McCarthy on a platform in Wisconsin, my last act as treasurer of the Harvard Teachers' Union was to write a check contributing the union's remaining funds (about sixty dollars) to the Massachusetts Civil Liberties Union in memory of F. O. Matthiessen. The teachers' union died because we could not persuade any professor to accept its presidency for 1952–53. The officers decided unanimously to honor Matthiessen's memory and to donate our little treasury to the ACLU.

Both the decision to honor Matthiessen and the choice of the ACLU have an even more important place in my instructed memory than they had at the time I concurred in them. Within a year or two after my arrival at Stanford in 1952, the name of the Harvard Teachers' Union began to turn up in an increasing number of newspaper reports about "Communist cells" and "Marxist study groups" described in testimony before congressional investigating committees. It may well be that some of those reports accurately described what had happened in the union before the war. In the four years of my membership, however, the union functioned exactly as Matthiessen would have wanted—as an open society in which every member had an equal voice. Perhaps the decisions we made were too trivial for any Communists among the members to believe conspiracies were worth the trouble. Whatever their motives, every officer in 1952 approved giving our funds to the ACLU in Matthiessen's honor—giving the money to an organization that, although it had voted to exclude members of the Communist party from its own membership, was committed to defend everyone against encroachments upon the Bill of Rights.

A similar judgment stands as my considered view of Matthiessen himself. Even after I had learned a little about his secret life, his private grief, and the range of personal motives that must have inclined him toward egalitarianism, his scrupulous collegiality, and his gloomy reading of the Cold War—even then I could not deny his exemplary value. I could not accept the reductive interpretation in which some colleagues presumed to explain ethical decisions by pointing to depression or homosexuality. I had learned in the intervening years to make similar judgments about such different characters as Cotton Mather and Ernest Hemingway, both of whom, though personally much more obnoxious than I ever heard anyone say that Matthiessen was, managed in their best work to turn anxieties and afflictions into public service by writing prose that still has power to move us. Whatever demons possessed Matthiessen did not merely depress him. Nor did their torment issue in destructive alienation until he felt impelled to destroy himself. They propelled or provoked him into the community to do good, to help students, to reconcile historical scholarship, modern criticism, and just political action; to use inherited wealth and social standing, along with scholarly eminence and authority, in the service of brotherhood.

Samuel Eliot Morison

The strongest images of Samuel Eliot Morison in my memory present him in uniform, ready for vigorous action. Although I rarely saw him dressed differently from any other professor, the first energetic image had impressed me in 1941, five years before I met him: I had seen the eminent historian eating a sandwich at the lunch counter in Woolworth's. He wore riding breeches and boots, a hacking jacket, and a hard hat that looked to me like a derby. The incongruity of this costume in a five-and-ten-cent store between Harvard Square and Brattle Square was intensified by my naïve belief, as a freshman, that Harvard professors always wore suits or flannel slacks and always lunched at the faculty club. Five years later, Morison wore his naval uniform when he delivered the first lecture in his undergraduate course on early American history. I can still see his braided cap, the bill pointed 90 degrees to our left, on the desk behind which he stood as he advised the open-shirted veterans (some wearing Eisenhower battle jackets) that Harvard gentlemen and scholars wore coats and ties to class. And even now, when I visit Boston, I can see the late Admiral Morison in a fine bronze statue on Commonwealth Avenue. He is seated in the relaxed but eager posture of a commander who peers ahead at the sea from under a long-billed cap like the one that Admiral Bull Halsey made famous.

These images do suggest Morison's personal and scholarly character. The man who still remembered in his eighties his boyhood resentment of long curls and a Lord Fauntleroy suit was also a lifelong admirer of the historian Francis Parkman. Shortly before World War II, Morison had emulated Parkman's insistence on studying the sites of historical action. Morison had used Christopher Columbus's log in a sailing expedition that retraced the great admiral's first voyage to America, and he had topped his prize-winning *Admiral of the Ocean Sea* by winning an assignment that Parkman would have coveted. As historian of American naval operations during World War II, Morison had been free to observe virtually any action he chose. He had witnessed some of the major battles described in his fourteen-volume history of the naval war, and he was writing that history when I was enrolled in his graduate seminar.

With admiration, then, but not without a certain unearned condescension, those of us who were students of literature and intellectual history, or committed to economic interpretation or social perspectives such as the history of immigration, considered Morison slightly old-fashioned. Surely we noticed that Perry Miller and Thomas H. Johnson had dedicated their innovative anthology of early New England literature to Morison, and that Morison had written several volumes demonstrating his mastery of intellectual issues in colonial New England and in the history of Harvard College. Nor did I underestimate the value of his fluency in Latin and Greek. Yet my friends and I revered him chiefly as a narrative historian who defended the importance of literary style in history writing. I also admired the grace and vigor of his prose, although his rhetoric sometimes rose toward the swashbuckling tone (without the clichés) of Parkman's most energetic flights.

Energy, learning, and rigor distinguished Morison as a teacher of graduate students. His seminar differed sharply from Perry Miller's. Both made the production of an original scholarly paper the student's chief obligation; but whereas Miller dismissed the seminar on Hawthorne and Melville until the first of our papers was due, Morison designed his seminar to introduce us to a variety of skills. He took us down to the Massachusetts Historical Society, where he was engaged in editing the manuscript of William Bradford's history *Of Plymouth Plantation*. There he not only showed us how to read Bradford's handwriting and the peculiarities of other seventeenth-century holographs, but made several of us read a few lines aloud and discussed editorial principles and ways of detecting later interpolations in old manuscripts. He made a passionate and largely convincing plea for modernizing the spelling and punctuation of so classic a manuscript as Bradford's, but the main lesson of this visit was the complexity of historical editing. He showed us the map collection in Widener Library and introduced us to different kinds of projection and distortion in sixteenth- and seventeenth-century maps. It was during his discussion of Mercator projections that I addressed a question to him as "Professor Morison" and provoked the abrupt reply: "Don't call me Professor Morison; call me Mr. Morison or Captain Morison."

Morison invited us to sail around Clark's Island and into Plymouth Harbor in his own yacht—not to teach us how to sail but to illustrate the importance of specific geographical knowledge as a critical tool and as an aid to historical imagination. (I had sailed about that harbor several times with my elderly friend and employer Thomas Weston, class of 1895, who had already asked me to imagine what it must have felt like to approach Clark's Island in a sleet storm in 1620.) And he showed us several drafts of a passage from his own history in progress, with both factual and stylistic revisions, to demonstrate that careful writing is an essential part, rather than merely a welcome decoration, of a good historian's work.

In Morison's seminar as in Miller's, nonetheless, we had to learn by performing. Here again the senior scholar held us to a high standard and apparently took some pleasure in enforcing it. Each of us had to choose two assignments from a sheaf of thin strips fanned out on the seminar table at the first meeting. For my major project I was relieved to see that nobody else wanted the slip that said "The Mathers' Influence on the Salem Witchcraft Trials," for I felt slightly less insecure with a topic that had at least some connection to literary figures. But while concentrating our major papers in the years between 1680 and 1693, each of us was also obliged to investigate and report orally on a disputed problem in the history of colonial exploration: the Kensington rune stone, supposedly inscribed by Norsemen in Minnesota several centuries before 1492; the Drake plate, found in California by a chauffeur four centuries after Sir Francis Drake had supposedly left it near the Golden Gate. Because I had already read George Bancroft's and Francis Parkman's histories, I chose the dubious exploits of one Father Louis Hennepin, a Recollet friar in La Salle's expedition to the Mississippi River who had published after La Salle's death a book claiming for himself the first discovery of the Mississippi's mouth.

These reports put a greater burden on Morison than on the speaker's fellow students. Perry Miller had required us to respond extemporaneously to each classmate's paper, after one designated critic had read us a formal review of it, and we were able to comply because we had all been reading Hawthorne and Melville throughout the semester. Morison's assignments virtually guaranteed that the auditors would have no independent knowledge of the Drake plate or the Kensington rune stone, for each auditor would have been preparing his own report on the search for the Northwest Passage or on the Zeno brothers. Polite, diffident questions did issue from one's fellow students, and we were all required to submit a few written comments on each report. Morison culled a line or two from each of these, read them to the next meeting of the seminar, and gave the speaker a copy of the excerpts. I have probably repressed more substantive comments, but I do remember a line that stood alone as one student's contribution to the page that Morison gave to me: "Mr. Levin has a pronounced lisp."

Performance by prospective teachers did include the quality of elocution, and the master did correct his apprentices' technique as well as their research. My respect for him deepened as he commented knowledgeably on the substance of one report after another. Even now, after four professorial decades have taught me that the person who chooses the topics and asks the questions may seem to be much more broadly learned than he actually is, I marvel at the range, the vitality, and the accessibility of Morison's knowledge. He was sixty-one in the autumn of 1948, and hard at work on his fourteen-volume *History of United States Naval Operations During World War II*. Of course our modern Thucydides had more help than his illustrious predecessor—a staff of naval personnel and a full-time secretary. But his scruples about first-hand geographical knowledge propelled him into flights all over the world, in naval aircraft much slower than modern jets. As I began my report to the seminar on Father Hennepin, for example, Morison covered a large yawn and excused himself: "If I yawn or nod a bit," he said, "it won't be because I am bored. I've just returned from the Aleutian Islands." He had taken two twenty-hour flights, each one across three time zones, in the four days since our last meeting. Yet his questions about Hennepin were as acute as if no other subject had occupied him in recent years. When I cited a clever skeptic's calculation that the fastest Olympic crews of the 1930s would have needed extraordinarily good luck (and unflagging strokes through day and night) to match the pace at which Hennepin must have rowed upstream for several hundred miles, Morison honked his nasal laugh in approval. Immediately after I had finished, however, he asked a sharp question about the skeptic's computations and a detail I had not mentioned in Hennepin's book.

Morison's insistence that William Bradford's spelling and punctuation should be normalized for the modern reader did not mean that he expected us to modernize seventeenth-century prose in our scholarly papers. Perhaps because his private secretary, Miss Card, was admirably efficient, he did not warn of one hazard that nearly sank my own ungainly bark. My paper on the Mathers ran to more than fifty double-spaced pages, with many quotations from the seventeenth-century texts. By the time I had completed the paper, near the end of my first term as a teaching fellow, I was obliged for the first time to hire a typist to prepare the final copy.

The typist was experienced in typing papers for Harvard undergraduates. When she returned the paper to me on the evening before my deadline, she remarked on my peculiar spelling. She was one of those helpful souls who corrected undergraduates' spelling and grammar. Besides "correcting" all the strange spelling and capitalization in my seventeenth-century quotations, she had sometimes revised my own prose, as in this obscure sentence: "Five days later Deliverance Hobbs confessed." My typist had never seen the name "Deliverance"; she substituted an elegant exclamation—"Five days later deliverance!"—began a new sentence with "Hobbs confessed," and carried on from there. I knew that Morison expected every quotation to be exact. With the help of my noble friend and fellow seminarian Jim Early, I was able to restore the original peculiarities, and Morison graciously accepted my apology and my messy typescript. He did not spare me a Matherian admonition concerning the unauthorized emendations we ought to expect from typists and publishers' editors.

By his example, then, and in his criticism of our own work, the master taught precision and fairness. He was eighteen years older than Perry Miller, and (concurrently with Barrett Wendell, George Lyman Kittredge, and Kenneth Murdock) he had been advocating sympathetic understanding of the New England Puritans before Miller arrived at Harvard. In the late 1940s hints of a friendly rivalry entertained us, when Morison remarked offhand in an undergraduate lecture that *some* scholars squander too much time on theological disputes and Miller retorted from his own podium. But the differences in emphasis proved to be complementary. Morison was better versed in the theology than either Murdock or the late Wendell, and perfectly willing to help us write about ideas. He simply let us know that his own inclination (and the historical fortune that had offered him the naval history) led him now to emphasize action and character. Those of us who read his *Builders of the Bay Colony* (1930) saw that he skillfully delineated religious issues and a variety of individual lives, that he strove to represent those characters as fully human beings, and that (despite his reference to social history as "so-called history") his sense of cultural history was broad for the times.

In preparing us for the profession, Morison did not neglect our own humanity. This cool, stiff Brahmin spoke earnestly to the seminar about our extracurricular lives and his own. We must not neglect our families, he said. We should all become life members of the American Historical Association as soon as we possibly could. We must resolve not to work all the time. His one great regret was that he hadn't spent enough time with his family; not until his wife had died, he told us, did he understand how severely limited one's life is. "Don't work all the time," the widower said again. "Take at least one month off every summer. Go to your cabin in Maine!"

He could not have known then that he had nearly another thirty years to live, or that he would survive a second bride, whom he met and married soon after our seminar had ended. His abundant publications during the next twenty-five years might have misled readers to believe that he continued to work all the time—if the society pages in Boston's newspapers had not printed photographs of the captain (later, the admiral) and his Priscilla dancing in one ballroom or another. Surely, too, the man who commanded me to go to my cabin in Maine would have understood my having occupied instead the chauffeur-gardener's cottage adjoining my employer's garage in Watch Hill, Rhode Island. Jim Early and I laughed privately over Morison's apparently unimaginative assumption that any of us could afford to own a summer cottage. Not until recently did it occur to me that Morison may have understood better than we the likelihood of our becoming moderately wealthy.

Morison did not engage us in discussions of contemporary politics. What we knew of his passionate commitment to the extracurricular life of his time was limited to his participation in the war. But he did propose as a topic for a paper in his undergraduate course the question, "Was Roger Williams a democrat?" One of my politically active classmates chose that topic, visited Morison's study in Widener Library to discuss his prospective paper, and then dared to inquire into Morison's own political affiliation. Morison pointed to an autographed picture of Franklin D. Roosevelt on the wall and said, "There's the Great Sachem himself."

Mixed though it surely was with strong egalitarian convictions, Morison's patrician heritage had a special meaning for his historical studies of New England. The location of his house in Brimmer Street meant nothing to his work on the naval history, but I could see that in his unostentatious way he took as much pleasure in sharing the tradition with us as we did in observing it. His affection for Parkman, William H. Prescott, and Henry Adams, his great nineteenth-century predecessors, had other roots than sturdy professional respect. These historians or their parents or grandparents were the Morisons' neighbors. Each of them had worked out his own relation to the early American past—Adams and Parkman completing their masterpieces in 1891 and 1892, respectively, when Morison was a child. When invited to the house itself, I had these connections in mind. As the child or grandchild of immigrants, I was moved by the thought of a tradition that included both the place and the efforts of several generations to write about it. And I could see that Morison, whose interest in sea power and naval history had been stimulated by his early reading of A. T. Mahan, was completely free of Mahan's virulent "Teutonic" infection.

Our visit to the house in Brimmer Street turned out to have a significance that was more antiquarian than historical. I don't know whether Morison contrived similar occasions in other years, but I can testify that the celebration at which we were present in 1949 gave me new insight into a historian's relation to his own time and his past. Perhaps the invitation did identify the occasion; as my memory preserves the event, my wife and I set out merely to attend a reception in a professor's house. We were surprised to discover that a ceremony had been planned. Morison and his daughter, who served as his hostess until he remarried, greeted us and ushered us into a drawing room upstairs, where we met my classmates and noticed that several students from Morison's undergraduate class in naval history were gathered close to the piano. Several older people were present—among them a businessman named Mark Bortman; a woman (or was it one of the students in naval history?) whom Morison identified as a descendant of John Dickinson, author of *Letters from a Pennsylvania Farmer;* and a Miss Burke, whom Morison tied (with a mock challenge flung at the Dickinson family) to *her* ancestor, Edmund Burke. One of my classmates told me about a middle-aged man who had not been introduced; upon inquiry the man had said he was a private detective, and that he was present to make certain that the Liberty Bowl didn't disappear.

We had been invited to celebrate the return of Paul Revere's Liberty Bowl to Boston. A committee chaired by Mr. Bortman had raised the money to buy the silver bowl from a private owner in New York for the Boston Museum of Fine Arts. Morison was a jovial master of ceremonies. Having introduced the Dickinson-Burke rivalry and Mr. Bortman, he reminded us that Revere had dedicated the Liberty Bowl to "the glorious NINETY-TWO"—the large majority in the Massachusetts legislature who in 1768 defied "the Menaces of Villains in Power" by voting "NOT TO RESCIND" a circular letter of protest against British policy. Morison told us that some of the men in his undergraduate class had rehearsed the Liberty Song, that they would now sing it for us, and that we were welcome to join in the refrain:

> Our weapons are ready—
> Steady, boys, steady—
> Not as slaves but as freemen
> our money we'll give!

After several hearty choruses, we moved into the dining room to drink a toast.

There Morison pointed out the gleaming Liberty Bowl on a linen-covered pedestal in the center of the table, and he announced that we were about to drink from the punch bowl of his ancestor Harrison Gray Otis a rum punch that had been mixed according to an eighteenth-century recipe. (My memory tells me Morison said that Otis had drunk the punch in this very room, but sober history says that Brimmer Street would not have been filled in soon enough.) Here again our jovial host allowed himself a little badinage about the descendants of Dickinson and Burke. When we all had full cups, we raised them and gave a rousing response to Morison's eighteenth-century toast: "To the Glorious Ninety-two!"

Back to the drawing room we went for some more refreshments and conversation. After a few minutes Mr. Bortman asked for our attention and announced that he wanted to present a little gift. His opening clause made me apprehensive, but he came through with a moving little speech, which I can only paraphrase after quoting the first five words: "When I was a lad . . ." Growing up as a Rumanian immigrant, he said, he had admired popular heroes like Babe Ruth, but in trying to learn about the history of his country he had found a different kind of hero in the young Harvard historian who made that history live, whether in the voyage of Columbus or the lives of the men who built the Bay Colony, or the story of the first American college. He said he felt honored to be able to return the Liberty Bowl from New York to its proper home, and that it was an even more satisfying privilege to honor Samuel Eliot Morison, his favorite historian, with an exact replica of Paul Revere's bowl.

We all applauded as he gave Morison the silver bowl, and again after Morison's gracious, brief reply. Under cover of the applause Miss Burke, who stood next to me, expressed some indignant perplexity. "Well, I should like to know whether I have been drinking punch in the presence of the Paul Revere Liberty Bowl or a mere replica!" I don't know whether she ever learned the answer.

The party did not end for us students until we had visited Morison in his library. There he gave each of us an autographed copy of his commemorative volume *The Glorious Ninety-two,* shook our hands, and (not rudely but decisively) bade us a good afternoon.

Let me be explicit about the resonance of that afternoon, in the context of my entire experience of Morison, as memory has often rerun the tape in the last forty years. Morison impressed me as a man who lived harmoniously in his historical place. He neither flaunted nor apologized for the Harrison Gray Otis punch bowl. He stood there in his unique relation to the recipe, the house, and the bowls; he made us students, the Burke-Dickinson descendants, and Mark Bortman welcome in our respective connections to the place and to our host. When Morison's historical work involved his regional and familial heritage, he seemed unabashed in acknowledging his perspective. His personal engagement in the histories of Columbus and the modern American navy was even stronger. Bold action, exploration, and vigorous narrative stirred him as the historian's most precious opportunities.

Besides his acceptance of his historical position, Morison's reception has come to illustrate for me the one quality for which I remember him most gratefully: his delight in his subject. All my best teachers expressed great affection for their work. Perry Miller showed the exaltation of pure scholarly delight when he delineated paradoxes or exploded misinterpretations that had become standard. The spirit of joyous scholarship glowed most happily in Oscar Handlin's face when Handlin posed an ingenious question which seemed to open a new perspective. Frederick Merk's high voice rose to an ecstatic squeal when he described the overflow of Henry Wallace's "ever normal grainery" into midwestern schoolhouses. I cannot say that Morison's zest was any more intense than theirs; it seems to me now to have been more pervasive, ranging from the antiquarian and genealogical lore of the punch bowl to the voyages of Columbus and the Battle of Midway in World War II. I heard that gusto in our host's remarks about Otis, Revere, Dickinson, and Burke; any reader could see it in the very footnotes to Morison's history of Harvard College and his edition of William Bradford.

Of course Morison was also sympathetically critical of my work in his seminar, and he urged me to choose a historical controversy for my doctoral thesis. He gave special encouragement not only to my interpretation of the Mathers but to my construction and execution of a narrative. Two years later, when I was actually choosing a subject for my thesis, he tried to dissuade me from writing on the New England romantic historians. "Write history, not criticism," he said. His own admiration for Parkman and William H. Prescott led him to review some modern editions of their work, and he had written a pamphlet on "History as a Literary Art," emphasizing narrative again. As a young man he had even been bold enough to tell Henry Adams that Adams's masterpiece was not *Mont-St. Michel and Chartres* (Adams's favorite) but the *History of the United States*. Morison simply could not endorse my argument that my projected work would be classifiable as both history and criticism. I do not regret my choice, but I certainly had Morison in mind when I decided in 1960 to write a narrative of Cotton Mather's life, and I am sorry that the book was not published until two years after Morison's death in 1976. Surely Morison would have been pleased to see, just thirty years after the seminar, and just three centuries after Mather became the youngest graduate of Harvard, that yet another student had turned to writing narrative after all.

Thomas Weston

CLASS OF '95

On my way to a party celebrating a relative's hundredth birthday a few years ago, I tried to remember whether I had known any other centenarians. The closest I could come to the magic number was my brief employment in 1941 and 1942 by a Mr. Fay, who at ninety-eight hoped to become the oldest living graduate of Harvard College, but who had died before reaching one hundred. Since I was sixteen when I began to work for him, he might as well have been 198 years old on those Monday and Thursday afternoons when I would call for him at the Brattle Inn, just off Brattle Square. And since my age had been emphasized as a major reason for my assignment to chauffeuring, rather than more lucrative employment, by the Student Employment Office, which could not assign anyone under eighteen to work in defense plants, I was acutely conscious of the fourscore and two years that separated me from Mr. Fay. At the Brattle Inn I would pick up the keys to his 1940 Ford, bearing license number 1869 to commemorate the year of his graduation from Harvard. I would bring the car over from Mrs. McCarthy's Brattle Street Garage and would take Mr. Fay for a ride—in the autumn for a look at the foliage and then a visit to his wife in the Peter Bent Brigham Hospital; during the next spring and autumn, to visit her grave in the Mount Auburn Cemetery, where he showed me his own tombstone beside hers, with his inscription already in the stone beneath a quill and scroll: "He was a versatile fellow."

Fortunately for me he was also an agreeable fellow, and as reasonable as he was adventurous. When his wife died, he decided that he should learn to drive for himself again, for I was available only two afternoons a week and would be joining the army air force at the end of the autumn term. I agreed to teach him. For safety's sake he chose the untraveled roads of the cemetery for his lessons. He made some progress, but we were foiled by two habits that he could not overcome. Because he could not hear very well or because his feet were relatively insensitive, he always raced the motor; and because he claimed that in his 1915 Buick the lowest gear had been on the lower right and the highest two on the left, he tended to start out in high gear and to try shifting into reverse after his abused Ford, bucking all the way, had somehow gathered a little speed.

Usually we stalled when he unintentionally started out in high gear, and when we did not the greatest danger was usually no more than that the bucking might damage one of his aging joints. By the third lesson he was forgetting less often, and I began to hope until, near the end of that afternoon, he nearly killed us both. He had completed three cycles in a row without a mistake, except for some unexpected lurching when he misused the clutch pedal. At the end of the third cycle we stopped just beyond the top of a little hill. He used the hand brake, shifted into neutral, then down into what he thought was first, raced the motor, released the brake, and slowly let up the clutch pedal. When the clutch engaged, the car leaped forward with a roar, and we went bucking down the hill. I urged him to shift into second. He jammed down the clutch pedal and thus shot us forward at even greater speed as he moved the screaming gear shift violently to the left and up toward the position for reverse. The stick of course jumped back into the neutral position, and we rolled in what we then called free wheeling toward a mausoleum at a bend in the road near the bottom of the hill.

Mr. Fay froze, clutching the wheel in what I feared was a death grip. I managed to nudge his right leg off the accelerator and to get my left foot onto the brake pedal, but against his resistance

I could not turn the steering wheel soon enough to keep the car on the road. We ended up on the grass, with the front bumper resting against the corner of the mausoleum, a slight dent in the bumper and a small chip in the stone.

It took me fifteen minutes to ease the car up out of the soft grass and onto the road, while Mr. Fay caught his breath and rested in the passenger's seat, but it took me no time at all to persuade him to abandon his quest for a new license. "I fear it's true," he said, "that you can't teach an old dog new tricks."

I did find myself teaching a more talented geriatric pupil twelve years later, after I had gone to Stanford as an instructor in English, but again the practical benefits were limited. Mrs. Albert L. Guerard, then in her late seventies, had learned from her son, one of my Harvard teachers, or else I had told her in one of her intense but delightful interrogations about what my wife and I had been doing in the years before we came to Stanford, that in my freshman year I had for several months worked as a car parker in the Motormart, an eight-story parking garage in Boston. When Mrs. Guerard summoned me for help, I thought of the car that Claude Rains had supposedly driven in the film version of *The Invisible Man*. Never a tall woman, Mrs. Guerard was so tiny in her last five or ten years that one did not see her head above the steering wheel when one saw her car approaching on the campus. One saw her light blue Buick rolling slowly along, the top of the steering wheel moving back and forth; only as one came abreast of her did one see her white head and her intense eyes peering through thick glasses at the small section of blue sky and distant road between the upper rim of the steering wheel and the lower edge of the windshield.

My assignment was to help her improve her parallel parking, so that she might pass the test for renewal of her driver's license. When I arrived at the Guerards' house on the Stanford campus, Mr. Guerard was placing some large coffee cans sixteen feet apart to mark the area in which the Buick would have to be parked. He had filled the cans with sand and had planted a four-foot stick in each one so that in order to pass the test the car would have to go around the front stick and stop short of the one in the rear. I demonstrated the technique once for my attentive pupil, urging her to use the power steering and light touches on the brake pedal so that the car would move very slowly, and to turn the front wheels as much as possible in the shortest linear space. When she got behind the wheel, she started smoothly from the parking place, circled through a neighbor's driveway on the left, pulled up abreast of the imaginary car, backed in smoothly without touching either of the sticks or coffee cans, and thanked me heartily, if breathlessly, for having shown her the importance of slow speed in parking. She said she would practice a few more times while the sticks were in place, but she insisted that I run along and get back to my academic work.

On the day of the test I telephoned to find out how she had done. "Oh, it went perfectly," she replied, "just as well as in my first effort with you last week." She paused so long that I thought she had finished, but as I started to speak she continued: "Only one thing went wrong. After I had parked so beautifully, the examiner told me to drive out and take him around the block to the right. Breathless with the effort and the excitement, I said, 'Young man, do you mind if I rest for two or three minutes?'" She passed the test but was restricted to a radius of five miles from her home.

The most energetic elderly person of my acquaintance needed no instruction in driving. Although hard of hearing and no longer keen of sight, Thomas Weston, of West Newton and Duxbury, Massachusetts, regularly drove his own car in the fierce traffic of suburban Boston and the South Shore, and he could labor doggedly at lifting, carrying, sawing for as much as half an hour after my strong young friends and I had been compelled to rest. He was seventy when I first met him, seventy-four when Pat and I moved into his house as housekeeper and companion, and seventy-seven when we left his house for my first teaching appointment in California. His Harvard class was that of 1895, fifty years earlier than mine, but down to the day of his death in his mid-eighties he maintained a vigorous interest in the young. He delighted in their company, and he sought to understand their ideas and, when he could, to join in their activities.

Pat and I met Judge Weston through his children. His eldest daughter had served as a counselor at an American Youth Foundation camp in New Hampshire, where Pat and the youngest of the three Weston daughters had been campers. The bonds had grown closer when Pat managed, unintentionally, to infect not only that eldest daughter but a large section of a Bryn Mawr dormitory with the mumps during an ill-timed visit to the campus in 1940. The permanent friendship was sealed the next summer by Pat's service, just after she had graduated from high school, as an *au pair* in the Weston household in Duxbury while Mrs. Weston was convalescing. In return for room, board, and the frugal stipend of six dollars a week, Pat helped with the cooking for five or ten people, swept out the house, and sometimes mowed the grass. Her eyes still shine with pleasure forty-nine years later when she describes that summer as it has become fixed in her memory: "I went sailing at high tide and clamming at low tide, and happily worked in between."

She remembered Judge Weston as excellent company. She spoke of him so warmly that I felt acquainted with him before I had actually met him. Thalia, his youngest daughter, was working at Harvard when I returned to my undergraduate studies there after the war, and Pat and I were soon invited to a Sunday dinner at West Newton.

I remember that first Sunday afternoon in the dining room of the West Newton house better than the hundred or more we spent there between 1949 and 1952. With the chandelier turned on and the bay windows letting in some sunlight, the dining room was the only bright room on the first floor of a very dark Victorian house. The round mahogany table had been extended to accommodate the guests, and I noticed on the hearth a plaster-of-Paris dog. The table was dominated by a large leg of lamb or mutton (bought, I later learned, at the Faneuil market in Boston on Judge

Weston's way home from work). When the judge said grace, I heard him intone for the first time the same words that I was later to hear spoken in precisely the same way more than a thousand times: "We thank Thee—our Father in Heaven—for this food —prepared for us.—May we receive it with grateful hearts—for Christ's sake—amen." And when he rose to carve the leg of lamb I heard for the first of dozens of times his ironic introduction to carving: "A good carver never stands up." By watching him at that table during the next several years, I learned how to carve a leg of lamb and a turkey. Although his personal style could never be successfully imitated, I hope that I also learned from him something about how to preside as a host, and about how the old might welcome the young.

He was just under six feet tall, now somewhat stooped forward from the waist but straight in that deviation from the perpendicular. His shoulders sloped away from his neck as if they had never been squared, so that it was hard to imagine, when he told some of his favorite anecdotes about his service in the militia during the policemen's strike in Governor Calvin Coolidge's day, how this soldier had ever stood at attention. He had a plodding walk that always made me think, when we worked together, of Captain Ahab's fixed and forward dedication, though of course with none of Ahab's fierceness. He had a pleasant face, close-clipped gray hair parted at the side and brushed forward, a thick gray mustache, a large black mole on one temple, a hearing aid in one ear. Before he spoke he would often run his tongue over his front teeth. He said he could not carry a tune, but he had a strong, clear baritone voice, with a fine ear for the rhythms of public speech, so pleasant that I never tired of hearing him tell the same anecdotes at the table for new guests, or sometimes for those who had heard them once or twice before but whose conversation made the retelling appropriate.

On that first Sunday, for example, he learned that I had been reading about a nineteenth-century minister named Lyman Beecher, father of Henry Ward and Harriet. The meal over, Mr.

Weston pushed back his chair, crossed his legs, rearranged his napkin after daubing his lips with it, and said, "You know, Dave, Henry Ward Beecher was not afraid to use dramatic effects when he preached in his Plymouth church in Brooklyn. One day he called the sexton into his study before the service and handed him a dove. 'Near the end of my sermon,' he said, 'I will look up to heaven, raise both hands, and call out, "And the dove descended!" I want you to be waiting in the belfry. When you hear me say those words, please release this dove and let it fly about the church.'

"Well, the sermon developed with great power, and at last Mr. Beecher arrived at the climax. He lifted both his hands and cried, 'And the dove descended!'" Here Mr. Weston looked up to the imaginary belfry and raised both hands, flipping his palms upward and outward as he raised his voice and then waited a moment before repeating both the gesture and the words. After another pause he lifted his hands again and spoke in a voice that thundered impatience and anxiety: "'And the dove descended!'

"At last a quiet voice spoke from the belfry"—and here our narrator's voice dropped to the matter-of-fact tone of the sexton: "'Mr. Beecher, the dumb cat has eat the bird. Shall I throw down the cat?'"

Judge Weston's interest in the young, genuine though it was, had a practical value as well. In the summer house that he left in trust to his daughters when he died nearly thirty years ago, a little sign still hangs on the kitchen wall: "Here *all* guests work." We came to know the family better not only at the annual Thanksgiving feasts, to which every guest brought an offering, but especially in working weekends at Duxbury. The house there would have been boarded up every winter, and Thalia's friends and several of mine would gather in Duxbury for a house party on Memorial Day weekend. It was on these occasions that I first saw our elderly friend outwork us—carrying the heavy shutters from the house to a loft in the barnlike garage, digging to prepare the vegetable garden, rolling the clay tennis court while several of us young men debated over how to lay down the tapes in the correct dimensions. Once in a hurricane that struck the coast while Pat and I were living with the Westons, his sailboat was blown onto the beach, and he and I went to retrieve the mushroom anchor, which must have weighed well over one hundred pounds. We carried it several hundred yards along the beach at low tide, struggling against the wind that not only resisted us but also stung us with pellets of find sand. I was twenty-five at the time, but I had to break my resolution that I would go on walking until my seventy-seven-year-old coworker conceded his own need for a rest.

Late in October, then, we would board up the windows, carry the rowboat up to the garage, beach the heavy raft, and then remove the stairway that gave us access to the beach. It was a happy exchange of labor and friendly companionship for good company and recreation, and since our elderly friend worked right along with us we could hardly resent the occasional miscalculation in which he gave thrift more value than safety. Once he asked me to invite two strong young friends to Sunday dinner so that we might help his brother-in-law, William Loring, to move a refrigerator. After the four of us, with Uncle William merely supervising because he had once suffered a heart attack, had wrestled clumsily with that bulky load, Judge Weston admitted that it would have been wiser to hire a moving company. I agreed the more emphatically because I knew that the refrigerator had come to Uncle William as a great bargain from an estate that Judge Weston was settling, but I am sure that the actual cost was virtually irrelevant to the judge's thinking. He simply believed that friends should always cooperate to avoid unnecessary spending.

During the years before we moved into their house, Mrs. Weston was obviously declining. We could see her drift into a blank reverie during a large dinner party at Thanksgiving or on a Sunday, and she would tell the same guest two or three times within half an hour that her middle daughter had moved out to Oakland, California, "on the toe of the continent." Sometimes Mrs. Weston would tune her violin after dinner during one of our visits, or she would sit down in the music room to play the organ, pumping the pedal as moths flew out of the case. But she would never play more than a few notes on either of the instruments. She showed us some of her poems, which Pat remembered having typed during her first summer in Duxbury. Mrs. Weston was evidently restricted to nostalgic memories in her effort to keep her artistic life going.

Her vagueness and unpredictability were excruciating for her husband. He could escape the household every weekday by going down to his law office in the firm of Weston, Patrick, and Church, but she could not safely be left alone all day. At dinner, which on weekdays was indifferently prepared by an elderly, irascible cook, Mrs. Weston's unrelieved conversation must have been unbearable for her alert husband. When the cook quit and then Thalia, the last daughter remaining in New England, moved to California with her husband, some drastic change had to be made. Perhaps as a trial, Pat and I were invited to spend the month of August with the Westons in Duxbury, where none of their own children were able to be present at the time. We found that we loved the old people and the place: from the "mullet drawers," which would spill all the silverware on the floor if an unsuspecting poor fish pulled them too vigorously, to the wicker chairs, the moth-eaten head of a deer above the fireplace, the picture of "Two Members of the Temperance Society"—two horses drinking water from a trough—in the dining room, the lawn that sloped down to Brewster's Bluff, fifteen feet above the beach. When we were invited to live with the Westons throughout the year, we found the offer irresistible.

Unless we accepted, it seemed likely that the house in West Newton would have to be sold and that Mrs. Weston might even have to be moved to a nursing home. But of course our motives were not disinterested. Before the war we had both accumulated debts for the college expenses beyond our capacity to earn. The two thousand dollars that we still owed might be paid back out of the stipend from my teaching fellowship if our room and board should cost us nothing for the next two or three years. We had also been told by a gynecologist that if we wanted to have a child we should have one soon. When Judge Weston accepted that likelihood with his usual hospitality, we agreed to move to West Newton in September.

By the standards of the 1980s that house was immense. Darkened by a verandah and by brown, woven grass paper on the walls, the living room was not much used. We had our breakfast and dinner punctually at seven and six, respectively, in the dining room, then did the dishes (with Pat washing and Judge Weston helping me to dry them) in the butler's pantry and the pots and pans in the kitchen pantry (on the opposite side of the kitchen). After dinner the two men would climb to the billiard room on the third floor for one or two games. Sometimes Mrs. Weston would join us. Increasingly uncertain about which of the two white balls used in the game was the cue ball, she would whistle vaguely as she deliberated. I soon learned to distinguish her tactical deliberations from her absentmindedness, and I loved to see some of her old certainty return when at last, having identified the cue ball and chosen her shot, she would grasp her ivory-handled cue in her right hand and form a perfectly firm bridge with her left. After the billiard game, which usually lasted about an hour, I would go to my study in one of the two small rooms at the head of the servants' stairs above the kitchen. If I had only reading to do, I would sit with Pat in our tiny living room, which we had refurbished with some cheap paint and our own few pieces of furniture. Here, when at home on Saturday night, we would receive through the open register the full aroma of the codfish cakes that Judge Weston would prepare for his Sunday breakfast, the only meal at which Pat was not expected to appear. (During our first year Thursday was the cook's night off, but unless we had some special plans Judge Weston needed us to help get his wife into the car and to keep some sort of conversation going at the table in the plain little café to which they always went.) The Westons retired to their separate rooms at about 9:30, but two hours later we almost always found Mrs. Weston fully dressed and puttering at her dresser when we went through the large front hall to our own spacious bedroom in the front part of the house.

It was a mark of the household's thrift that Mrs. Kiley, the cleaning woman, came in only once a week to clean that big house and do the laundry. It was a sign of the judge's charm that the woman who was overburdened with that weekly task still revered him. She was a tall, skinny woman, the widow of a retired policeman; we guessed that she was at least seventy-five years old. Her routine did not change during our first year in the house, although Pat tried to show her how she could save labor and increase her efficiency. Mrs. Kiley distrusted all electrical appliances. In the basement she washed the Westons' sheets and the judge's shirts by hand, scrubbing them on a board in the tub right next to the Bendix washing machine. She used an old Bissel carpet sweeper, rather than our electric Hoover, to clean the Persian rugs in the living room. And she mopped under Judge Weston's bed and then scrubbed the hearth in his bedroom. Gradually, then, Pat found herself taking over the cleaning that Mrs. Kiley did not accomplish, for Pat could not stand to live in a dirty house and she hated to see the fine rugs riddled by carpet beetles and moths. Mrs. Kiley was with us only that one year. I felt guilty about our role in her dismissal, irrefutable though the evidence of her incompetence surely was, for it was not clear that anything was being done about her income. Eventually her place was taken by an elderly Finnish woman, Esther Jalonen, who was not only a dear soul but a marvel of efficiency.

During the academic year our routine encounters with Judge Weston centered in the dining room, the kitchen, and the pantry. At breakfast the *Boston Herald* always lay on the rug between his chair and mine. He would take up the paper after he had finished his egg, and he would hand me the front section as he began to read the sports and financial pages. The autumn months were the easiest on our breakfasts, for we could discuss the close pennant races between the Red Sox and the Yankees and then the World Series and the Harvard football games. We went together to all the games in the Harvard stadium, where I eventually learned not to shout but to applaud with the members of the 1890s classes who surrounded us.

But those were the years of the ex-Communist witnesses, the Hiss case, the loyalty oaths, and (eventually) Joe McCarthy; on many mornings the *Boston Herald*'s headlines provoked us to discuss politics rather than sports, and our discussions, sometimes heated, would then last throughout the drive to Harvard Square, where I would drop Judge Weston at the subway station before parking the car for the day. He was embarrassed by the tactics of the Committee on Un-American Activities, but as a Republican he generally agreed with the *Herald* that the actual Communists had to be ejected from the government and that the Democratic administration had too casually tolerated them. It cost him a powerful effort to endorse the Harvard administration's resistance to demands that radical professors be fired, but his loyalty to Harvard, to me, and to fair play enabled him to pay the price. He knew that I taught with John Ciardi, one of those whose dismissal had been called for, and that F. O. Matthiessen was one of my favorite teachers. Judge Weston accepted my defense of these men, even when he doubted their political judgment and my own, and I will never forget the sympathetic pain on his face on the morning that the *Boston Herald*'s banner headline reported Matthiessen's suicide. Both that sympathy and Judge Weston's indignation at breakfast the next day gave me the kind of support for which one is grateful in the very best of friends—a firm personal loyalty and imaginative understanding that can be relied on even when the friend cannot approve of one's ideas or actions.

The object of our indignation the next morning was a former sports columnist named Bill Cunningham. We had often enjoyed mock debates over this flamboyant writer's sports columns, colorfully overwritten and unfailingly arrogant. Specializing in verbal assaults on celebrated athletes and coaches, Cunningham had begun during World War II to use the bridge from sports to patriotism as an entry into political comments—most notoriously in an attack on Ted Williams's application for a draft deferment in 1942. By the time of Matthiessen's death in 1950, Cunningham had been regularly devoting entire columns to political matters. On the day after the suicide he published forty-five column inches on Matthiessen's alleged cowardice and a complete list of the thirty-four organizations to which Matthiessen had allegedly belonged despite their presence on the attorney general's list of subversive groups. Although in our political debates Judge Weston had often defended the attorney general's propriety in issuing those lists, he called that column of Bill Cunningham's obscene.

Our dinners were naturally less hurried than our breakfasts, and the conversations that revealed Judge Weston's character would usually begin with an inquiry about what amusement or instruction my day's work as a student or teaching fellow had produced. Not all the leather-bound sets of Jane Austen, Sir Walter Scott, William H. Prescott, and Francis Parkman in the Westons' library had uncut pages, and Judge Weston often used his membership in the Boston Athenaeum to check out books that I needed there. Even more lively than the questions about my reading in those volumes were his questions and anecdotes about American religious and political history. When I spoke of my readings in Congregational and Unitarian sermons, my irrepressible friend might retell the story of Henry Ward Beecher and the dove, or he might tell us about how the money from the Calvinist seminary at Andover had eventually gone to the Baptists' seminary in Newton, rather than to Harvard or other Unitarian divinity schools, according to the legal doctrine of *cy-pres*.

The best of these anecdotes were similarly political and comic not only in their amusing quality but also in the ironic discrepancy between pretense or expectations and the actual result. When I assigned *The Autobiography of Lincoln Steffens* to my Harvard freshmen, the judge told me of his own association with Martin Lomasny, the Boston boss from whom Steffens claims to have learned much about urban government. As a Republican member of the Massachusetts legislature, Thomas Weston had agreed to support a law making physical education in the public schools compulsory. Finding that groups he identified as "the Catholics" and "the Christian Scientists" had effectively blocked the legislation, he had gone to see the Democratic boss, Martin Lomasny, and had easily won his support, but with a proviso. "The Catholics," Judge Weston said, had opposed compulsory physical education for fear it might mean sex education in the schools; "the Christian Scientists" had opposed the requirement for fear that it might mean compulsory medical examinations. Lomasny agreed to deliver the Democratic votes in the legislature if the proposed requirement could be changed from "compulsory physical education" to "compulsory indoor and outdoor athletic sports and exercises." Thus the narrative of my elderly friend confirmed Lincoln Steffens's judgment that Lomasny's word, once given in a political negotiation, could be relied on, and that amateur reformers were sometimes foolishly stubborn. Judge Weston claimed that the lobbyists whose legislation he had agreed to support were irritated by the change in terminology; they had been fighting for years for compulsory physical education, he said, and they would not change the name. He told me that, for their own cause and because he too had given his word, he had decided to desert the reformers then, and that Lomasny had come through with the votes. What Lomasny had received in exchange the story did not say, and I did not ask.

My favorite among these stories would usually follow the tale about Lomasny. I believe I first heard this anecdote about Lomasny's successor, James Michael Curley, when I happened to remark that one of Mayor Curley's last official acts before beginning to serve his prison sentence in the federal prison in Danbury in 1947 had been to approve my appointment (along with a hundred others) as a playground instructor in Boston. As Judge Weston told the story, Curley's re-election to some office had once been challenged by a candidate who said Curley had fraudulently taken a civil service examination for a policeman. At a political rally a man in the audience had asked Curley bluntly about that accusation, and the angry crowd of Democrats in the hall had threatened the questioner and cried, "Throw him out!" Curley had allowed the anger to rumble for a few seconds, and then he had held up his hand in a gesture of tolerant resignation.

Judge Weston, of course, held up his own right hand as he reached this point in the story, and then he continued with his version of Curley's reply: "Now you remember, Dave, that James Michael Curley had a golden tongue and that it spoke in the accents of Harvard, although he never studied there. 'My friends,' Curley said, 'you must not deny this benighted man the greatest privilege that our Constitution allows even to fools, the right of free speech. Although his tone suggests that he asked his question maliciously, I shall be glad to answer it civilly. Yes, sir, I did once take an examination in a policeman's place. But that man was not just *a policeman*. He was the father of eight children and the husband of a lovely woman who had contracted tuberculosis and had to be sent to a sanatorium. That man had experience as a constable and as a deputy sheriff, but he had not had a long formal education and he was not experienced in taking examinations. I know that I broke the letter of the regulations when I took that man's place, but since I knew him to be competent, brave, and yes, needy, I was true to the spirit of the law, the heart of our system, and although I was technically wrong I would in the same circumstances do the same thing again. Let me assure you, moreover, that before the scandal was whipped up by my political opponents that man had a fine record as a brave policeman, protecting the lives and property of our citizens. He was truly one of Boston's finest.'

"Well, Dave, that crowd went wild over Curley's eloquent reply. He waved to them as they cheered, and then he left the hall, got into a limousine with the man who had asked him the offensive question, and together they drove off to the next rally."

Pat took even more delight in these conversations than I did. She had been fond of Judge Weston ever since her first summer at Duxbury, and now she had another reason to be grateful for the company whenever he or I came home. Especially in that first year, until our son was born in July 1950, Pat found the house gloomy and the companionship of poor Mrs. Weston and poorer Mrs. Kiley oppressive. She relieved the monotony by attending faculty wives' meetings at Harvard and by taking full advantage of the one weekday that Judge Weston would occasionally reserve for raking leaves on the ill-tended grounds at home or for driving through the splendid red and yellow foliage to Duxbury. She also poured her energy into the sewing and cooking she had not had time to do while working at the MIT wind tunnel, and we eagerly accepted Judge Weston's encouragement to entertain our young friends even when there was no heavy work to be done. Yet I could see Pat's face light up when the judge and I arrived at last for dinner, and she joined heartily in the dinner conversation.

In some ways Pat's life in those years must have been more difficult than that of other young women married to graduate students. Even before the war, however, it had become customary for both spouses to work. Charlotte Levenson worked in a laboratory in the Harvard Medical School, Faith Swerdlow in the Fogg Art Museum. Ann Early taught in the Concord High School, Ann Berthoff in Bradford Junior College. Helen McCormick and Jean Parrish opened a bookstore in Cambridge. Richard Wilbur and his wife solved the housing problem for a while by serving as house-sitters or caretakers, but without the domestic duties that Pat took on. Jane Marx and Valerie Lynn postponed their own study for degrees as psychiatric social workers until after their husbands were established in good academic posts.

In our academic generation, moreover, the enrollment of women in the American civilization program suddenly increased. Barbara Miller Solomon was a few years ahead of us. Barbara Myers, Elaine Ryan, Corinne Gilb, and several others formed the advance guard in a new corps being trained within a Faculty of Arts and Sciences that still looked like a male fortress. Some of these scholars and classmates' wives became our lifelong friends. Occasionally Pat might be bored by one of our literary arguments, or smilingly deflect a condescending question from a woman scholar who assumed that professional work was the only form of dignified labor. Pat knew, however, that they had their battles to fight against male complacency in the institution and against some of their own conflicting standards for professional and domestic fulfillment. She knew that we had freely chosen to live with the Westons for our own complex reasons, and that we both loved them and their children. We kept in touch with some of Pat's friends from the wind tunnel, and our many hours with the extended Weston family kept us aware, at least now and then, of other perspectives on academic life.

During our dinners at the house on Valentine Street, Mrs. Weston joined in the conversations, too, often to our delight even as we saw that what amused us irritated her husband, who surely remembered her command of an intellectual force that we could only imagine. Her comments at the table often came out of that past, a realm in which she had evidently been in charge of high culture. I remember that one of the subjects about which my Harvard and Radcliffe students had to write during our first autumn in West Newton was the controversy over Diego Rivera's mural in Rockefeller Center. The Rockefeller family had asked the painter to remove a head of Lenin from the mural, and he had refused, provoking the question of who owns a commissioned work of art. On six successive Tuesdays and Thursdays during the three weeks that my classes spent on these materials, Mr. Weston would ask how the discussion had gone, or what some of the students' papers had said. And on each of these occasions, as ingenuously as if the subject had never been mentioned until this moment, Mrs. Weston would speak precisely the same words, because she had heard of the seventeenth-century Spanish painter but not (apparently) of the twentieth-century Mexican: "Doesn't he spell his name Ribera, R-i-*b*-e-r-a?" Forty-eight hours later our explanations of variant spellings and of the distinction between *Lo Spagnoletto* in Naples and Rivera in Rockefeller Center would be as completely erased as if they had never been spoken. Mr. Weston's only comment on the repetitions would be a pained "No, Mother."

Besides companionship, then, our chief service to Mr. Weston was to ease the pain of his wife's predictable unpredictability. One of us could shorten the seemingly interminable delays by staying in the house to cajole her into leaving after her husband, waiting impatiently and sometimes leaning on the horn, had long since finished warming up the car. And when her forgetfulness produced real humor, our moderate laughter could occasionally temper his impatience. The approach of my birthday that first November led to a discussion, while I was in the kitchen scraping the garbage from the dinner plates, of the cake that Pat wanted to prepare secretly for me. The three of them were still talking when I came out of the pantry to serve the dessert and coffee, whereupon Mr. Weston hushed Mrs. Weston and she revised her sentence so that the birthday boy, the teacher of English composition, would not guess the secret: "Why don't we have an a-n-g-e-l cake?" Even the judge managed to smile.

Nor was Mr. Weston the only close associate who found the absentmindedness painful. Dr. Robinson, the family physician, knew of her unreliability as well as anybody else, but he too was sometimes deceived. One evening during a sleet storm, we were having our dessert in the dining room, and Mrs. Weston, whose appetite had remained hearty, had served herself a large portion of ice cream. It was nearly seven o'clock. Dr. Robinson, at the end of a long series of hospital rounds and house calls, burst into the vestibule, as he always did, without knocking, left his ice-covered umbrella in the stand in the foyer, marched past the statue of David and Goliath in the front hall, and stopped short, his raincoat dripping onto the rug, in the doorway to the dining room.

"Why Dr. Robinson, what a happy surprise!" Mrs. Weston said. "Take off that soaking coat and have some ice cream and coffee with us."

"What are you doing down here eating ice cream?" he demanded. "My nurse told me you had made an emergency call about another attack of angina."

"She must be mistaken. I did no such thing."

Dr. Robinson did not say good night. He turned and stomped out, closing the door smartly. He told us later that her angina was as genuine as her senility, but he said the knowledge only made him feel more helpless.

To complicate Mr. Weston's life and ours, there was another person who took a strong, intimate interest in Mrs. Weston's condition. Miss Grace Weston was five years older than her brother. His unpublished memoirs, which he wrote after we had moved to California, show that for years before he married in his mid-thirties Grace Weston had often accompanied him to dances and on overnight hiking parties in the White Mountains with groups of other young men and women. Seventy-nine years old when we settled in West Newton, Aunt Gee (pronounced with a hard *g*, as in Grace) sat as straight at the dining or bridge table as the most stringent governess would require a young lady to sit, and she looked out vigilantly for her brother's welfare. Her social life still took her on extended visits to other households up and down the coast of New England and New York, but whenever she was in town she dined with us on alternate Sundays, and on the other Sundays we joined her in the dining room of her apartment hotel in Newton Square.

Her attitude toward Mrs. Weston was conditioned by her own strength as well as by whatever rivalry she may have felt toward her beloved brother's wife. Although the two families got along well enough, it seemed likely to me that the Lorings had been wealthier than the Westons, and more interested in the performing arts than in hiking, gardening, or social dancing. One of Mrs. Weston's brothers had been a prominent banker, an uncle had been mayor of Newton, and her surviving brother, Uncle William, had been a painter and teacher at the Rhode Island School of Design. It almost seemed as if Aunt Gee, though correctly kind to her sister-in-law, had formed a moral judgment of her disability —as if the younger woman's susceptibility to arteriosclerosis followed logically from the preferences of her youth. In the years of our residence Aunt Gee was determined not to let her brother be dragged into imbecility by his wife's ailment, and so she resolved to complement his avid chess playing by teaching him to play bridge.

Pat and I figured in that design. On Sunday after Sunday during our three winters in West Newton, we would play bridge for an hour or two after the dishes had been washed in the house on Valentine Street, or after we had left the dining room for Aunt Gee's rooms in the Vernon Court apartment hotel. In the Westons' house Mrs. Weston would be free after dinner to amuse herself in the music room or in her own room upstairs, but in Vernon Court she would have to sit on the old loveseat, supplied with a magazine and a few chocolates, while Aunt Gee occasionally gave her a firm glance, and suggested an article to her, from her own position opposite Mr. Weston at the bridge table. There Aunt Gee gave her brother strong encouragement while introducing us all to the slogans and axioms of the game as she played it. The young man who neglected to draw trumps wound up walking the streets of London, she said a hundred times, and she always attributed the failure of a finesse to "hard lines." She would not proceed if the wrong person cut the cards, not until we had observed a ritual of correction. She supported her brother's loyal interest in the Boston Red Sox; although in those years she did not attend any games with us, she would turn on the radio during our bridge games in the last weeks of the season if the Red Sox were still in contention for the pennant.

I was surprised to learn, from a batch of Pat's old letters which her parents saved and recently returned to us, how often our friends had been allowed to join us for dinner in West Newton or in Duxbury. Although we paid for the food on those occasions, the Westons' participation in our young social life was remarkable. We entertained a family with three children; three of my four brothers and sisters and their spouses; a dozen fellow Harvard students; my mother; Pat's parents and (separately) two of her three sisters; my old freshman-English teacher; a classmate of my navigation class in the army air force; my Harvard and Radcliffe students, including a young black student from Alabama, whom Mrs. Weston welcomed on Thanksgiving by assuring him that now he was going to be introduced to a "genuinely *American* Thanksgiving"; the chairman of the Stanford English department, who had come to Cambridge on other business after my appointment to the Stanford faculty had been approved. (That eminent guest devoured eighteen of Pat's popover muffins at one dinner before laboring up to our sitting room for a private chat.) Mr. Weston was happier when these parties included bridge games, charades, billiards, or singing around the piano, than when (in his words) we just sat around and talked, but he always participated cheerfully, and he always retired discreetly in time to leave us alone with our guests. He was especially fond of our dear friends Robert Cross and Barbara Myers, and he was delighted to help us arrange a shower for them in West Newton a few weeks before their wedding.

With his own extended family, moreover, the celebrations were numerous, and the generations assembled in Duxbury, in West Newton, or at the Lorings' house in Newton Center. Before her labor pains began on the afternoon of our son's birth, Pat had roasted a leg of lamb for a party of fifteen in Duxbury, and our son spent his first two years in a large household that was alternately crowded and almost vacant. We celebrated Aunt Gee's eightieth birthday, Mr. Weston's seventy-fifth, and Uncle William's seventieth, as well as our son's first and my twenty-fifth. Except for the annual luncheon in the Toll House in Whitman, Massachusetts, to celebrate the birthdays of Uncle William and Mr. Weston, which fell within two days of each other in mid-August, all of these parties welcomed all the generations. The Westons and the Lorings took an affectionate interest in our son, and a high chair was always waiting for him at our table when we dined in Vernon Court. Since he loved dogs and, from the moment he learned to walk, would try to embrace any dog in sight, we were allowed to buy a puppy for him and to train her in the big house. We were all charmed by the child's habit of standing a few feet in front of

Mr. Weston's bee hives to watch the traffic entering and leaving them on a sunny day. Even after he was stung by a bee that had been trapped under his shirt, he would spend half an hour standing near the hive, singing quietly to the bees. Mr. Weston loved to watch him there, and of course Aunt Gee was delighted by the eighteen-month-old child's rendition, in perfect tune, of "Happy Birthday" on her eighty-first.

This is a memoir of exemplary qualities in an admirable man. Its validity does not require that he be portrayed as perfect or his household as idyllic. There were predictable clashes between our energetic child and Mrs. Weston. Before he could crawl or speak she would sometimes take his hands and sing in endless repetition, "How de do de do de do and how de do de do, and how de do and how de do and how de do de do . . ." until Pat could contrive to release him. After he learned to crawl and then to walk, Mrs. Weston would sometimes be found standing over him and saying, "No child, no no no no." Once he hurt her feelings by stealing a graham cracker from the dresser in her bedroom and devouring the cracker impishly in the doorway as she stood weeping in her room. Between the two families, moreover, some tension naturally developed concerning the rising cost of feeding us and the heavy burden of work that fell to Pat. Mr. Weston was not always willing to perceive the worsening condition of his wife, who became increasingly negligent about the cleanliness of her clothes and her person, and not all of his standard responses at the dinner table were so delightful as the ones I have cited. He sometimes embarrassed us and our friends by seeking to end a debate with the reminder that in his days at Harvard his classmates would always say, "If we can't agree on this issue, we can all agree about one thing: To hell with the Pope!" And although he was affectionately generous to a Catholic friend of Thalia's husband, welcoming him to the house even after Thalia and her husband had moved to California, Mr. Weston was obviously distressed when a Catholic family bought a house across the street. He feared that the next step would be to sell that house or another to a religious order, which might then establish a parochial school and lower property values in the neighborhood. Yet I thought then, and I still believe today, that if I should be fortunate enough to live into my seventies with a mind as open to new ideas and experience as his was, I would be a lucky man.

In his legal practice, however, Mr. Weston wanted as little variety, as little change, as possible. He had practiced law with his father, had spent some time in the state legislature, and had been appointed a judge in the municipal court for a few years. By the time we came along, he was working part-time in the firm that bore his family's name, but he wanted no cases except the settlement of estates. Certainly he wanted no trials.

Of the three most memorable cases about which he spoke to me, only one turned out as simple and respectable as he wanted his cases to be. That was the Plummer estate, the property of an eccentric who had ridden everywhere, even to the Boston Symphony, on an old bicycle until a few days before his death at the age of eighty-eight. Even here there were some peculiarities. A collection of hundreds of clean, crumbless, empty cartons which had once contained graham crackers was stacked in perfect order along two walls of the late Mr. Plummer's filthy apartment. Frightened of germs, Mr. Plummer had always used a cheap new fountain pen and had worn gloves when paying his bills, and yet the main rug in his apartment had not been cleaned, not even with a vacuum cleaner, for at least a decade. The new gas refrigerator that my friends and Mr. Weston and I helped Uncle William to move stood unused in the dust on the rug. It was when we wrestled the refrigerator out of its place that we discovered the true color of the dark brown rug—a bright orange. And since Mr. Plummer had been afraid to open many germ-bearing envelopes containing dividend checks and bills, the financial affairs of the estate were tangled.

The Plummer estate was successfully settled during our residence in West Newton, and I learned much from the resourceful way Mr. Weston solved the few problems he told me about, and from the attitude of tolerant comic acceptance that he took toward his late client's eccentricities. Of the other two anomalous cases that he discussed with me, he was able to keep only one under a semblance of control. This was the estate of a distant relative, an attorney, who in old age had mishandled funds entrusted to his care by a client. There could easily have been a scandal. The surviving beneficiaries of the trust were ready to take legal action to recover their property from the estate. Mr. Weston arranged a settlement by persuading some of the late attorney's heirs to make quiet restitution. No further harm was done. The man was dead. Why drag the family's name and his good reputation through the newspaper?

I have forgotten the name but not the circumstances in the case that taught me how little control even the most meticulous of counselors can exert over the human affairs in which he becomes engaged. Mr. Weston's client was a French immigrant who had adopted the two children of a sibling killed by the Germans in occupied France during World War II. Mr. Weston had agreed to represent the man in efforts to protect his interest in the mother's estate in France, and at dinner one night he had told me about the settlement of the case, noting some of the differences between French and Anglo-American law. One Sunday morning at about two o'clock we were all awakened by a telephone call, but Mr. Weston answered it and I did not learn until I came downstairs at ten that the call had come from the Newton jail. The client had been arrested for statutory rape and incest. His fourteen-year-old niece and adopted daughter had hanged herself and had left a note explaining why she could not bear to return to her home. The client had called his attorney, Thomas Weston. Mr. Weston had refused to represent him.

For months before we moved to California, the Weston daughters wisely urged their father to sell the house at 56 Valentine Street and move into a small apartment. Their mother's memory, they argued, was so unreliable now that the move from Duxbury to an apartment at the end of the summer would not be too painful for her. We had many discussions, when Mrs. Weston was not present, about clearing out the house in preparation for the big move. Mr. Weston suggested, for example, that Pat try to cook some of the eggs that had been put up in water glass in the basement during World War II, but after one look inside the barrels Pat had decided to leave the experiment to more adventurous cooks. Then Mr. Weston decided to give Pat for her birthday a set of the Weston family's dishes that had been stored in the closet under the front stairway. In looking for the dishes he found a carton containing the ashes of a former client whose will had stipulated that they be saved until his wife's death, whereupon the two sets of ashes would be scattered from an airplane above the Atlantic Ocean. The wife had died, but Mr. Weston had been unable to find her husband's ashes until he went looking for Pat's birthday gift.

He did sell the house when we left, to a buyer who agreed to accept the basement as it was, water glass, eggs, and all, if the billiard table was left in its room on the third floor. Poor Mrs. Weston could not move to the Vernon Court apartment-hotel with her husband, for her illness had developed into a paranoia that required her to be hospitalized. For nearly seven years, then, Aunt Gee had her belated victory, the company of her brother at dinner and at bridge, and she survived for several years after his death in 1959. We last saw her in the summer of 1961, when we arranged to take her out to dinner with our two children and to return her to the nursing home in which she spent her final years. I remember that she was sitting as erect as ever when we called for her, her head up and her eyes staring straight ahead. She remembered us cordially from nearly a decade before this visit, and she had already forgotten the visit of her niece just two days before ours.

I learned from Thomas Weston many things for which I remain grateful more than thirty years after our last meeting. Along with trivial pleasures like bringing a sailboat up to a mooring or digging clams, extracting honey, smoking out the bees, and playing chess, he taught me minor but interesting facts about the New

England history that I was studying. He took us sailing around Clark's Island, where the Pilgrims had first landed in Duxbury Bay, and he took us sailing up the tortuous Jones River, and told me the Pilgrims had named it for the Mayflower's captain "because of its circuitous ways." Since our friend was the fourth successive Thomas Weston after four successive Edward Westons, he also gave me a sense of the direct line, through eight generations, from the founding at Plymouth down to his own birth in 1875, his own presence sailing in the same bay in 1950. My studies in William Bradford's *History of Plymouth Plantation* helped me to understand why our Thomas Weston was glad he had not been descended from the Thomas Weston whose unreliability and financial demands had made life miserable for the Pilgrims in the 1620s.

But the most valuable gift he gave me, besides the experience of his friendship, was the example of openness in old age to new ideas and experience, a cheerful welcome to the young. He deserved the good fortune of his last years, the health that enabled him to travel about the world visiting his children—in California, where we saw him once again, in the Netherlands, and in Ohio. I have said that I would be lucky to have a mind as open as his was if I should live into my seventies. Anyone would be lucky, too, to die as Thomas Weston did at the age of eighty-four. During a chess game with his friends in the Newton Chess-nuts, he said that he felt tired, he lay down on a sofa, and he went to sleep.

Cornelia McLanahan Curtis

PORTRAIT OF A LADY

The chief exemplary quality that I found in Cornelia McLanahan Curtis (Mrs. F. Kingsbury Curtis), who employed me as a chauffeur-gardener in the summer of 1948, was a nearly perfect confidence in her personal and social identity. I saw the social part of that confidence shaken only once, under ambiguous circumstances which I shall describe later, and that one debatable lapse has more anthropological than ethical significance. I can say confidently that for me Mrs. Curtis exemplified delightfully, if sometimes comically, the message of Polonius, Popeye, and Ralph Ellison's Invisible Man: I am what I am.

The ethical significance of what Mrs. Curtis so confidently was depends on the historical circumstances of her class. The most memorable definition that I heard of her class came to me one day that summer in a pronouncement by the Scottish governess who had nurtured Mrs. Curtis's two daughters and at least some of the grandchildren. "Oh, Mr. McLanahan," she said to me when I asked what Mrs. Curtis's father had done for a living, "he was a gent'lman. He never worked a day in his life."

I assume that the late F. Kingsbury Curtis had worked many days in *his* life. Mrs. Curtis told me that her husband had been an attorney, that he had invested heavily in real estate in Florida, and that he had founded Tuxedo Park, New York. Certainly her two sons-in-law worked, one as an attorney and both as directors of corporations, and the grandson who was her husband's namesake became a physician. But all these men, too, were gentlemen, and the standards by which Mrs. Curtis lived included the best as well as some of the more frivolous values of northeastern American gentility.

In 1948 the middle-aged ladies and gentlemen in the family had more reason than my seventy-five-year-old employer ever acknowledged to be unsure of their status, or at least uncomfortable in it. Although they always treated my wife and me generously, our very presence on the family's summer estate complicated their lives in a way that their mother's generation could hardly have predicted. Pat and I didn't cause the uncertainty; our presence was a sign of uncomfortable times.

I was one of a succession of Harvard graduate students whom Mrs. Curtis hired to spend the summer working in Watch Hill, Rhode Island. It was Charles Sanford, my predecessor, who suggested that I apply for the job after he decided that he could not return to it for a second summer, and Charles warned me of a complexity which I recognized within two weeks of my arrival in Watch Hill. "There's a butler named Jerry who works for one of the daughters, Mrs. Lombard," Charles said; "a nice guy, out of the coal mines in Nova Scotia. You'll find him interesting to talk to, but he's a man on the way up, and he'll be watching you. He'll ask you a million questions, and he'll learn fast. He has a union background; the Lombards won't appreciate his eagerness to learn from you."

Jerry and his wife served all year as butler-chauffeur and housekeeper for the Lombards, who lived in Dedham and occupied one of Mrs. Curtis's two houses in Watch Hill every summer. These two servants had an infant daughter, about whose future Jerry expressed a passionately ambitious concern. In Mrs. Curtis's household, however, the servants were unmarried Irish women, Bessie the elderly cook and Mary the upstairs maid. In Mrs. Curtis's generation servants had regularly come from Ireland and had either stayed, like Bessie, as loyal spinsters or left the household to be married after a suitable replacement (often from the same family) had been found in the old country. By 1948 the number of servants had declined, but the relationship was still firm in the Curtis ménage, where Mary, in her twenties, would probably not stay much longer and Bessie, who had proudly brought over several of her family from Ireland to American prosperity, would surely remain until she retired.

Mrs. Curtis's Harvard students agitated this already bubbling mixture of duties, loyalties, and status. Unquestionably our charming employer loved having articulate young men to entertain her; she told happy anecdotes of her receptions for naval and army air force officers in her winter home in Florida, and she enjoyed calling me in for tea not only in her own house but also when she happened to swing the subject around to literature at someone else's tea. She was a small, handsome woman, small enough to curl up on the back seat of her Buick for a nap during some of our longer drives. She had a fine way of expressing innocent delight or naughty irony with her smiling eyes. The innocent delight would shine there when she would come out to her car and command me, in a voice that rose and fell as far as Eleanor Roosevelt's: "Now *close* that book and come *right* in, David; we're talking about *Littratyour!*" The irony would bring a little more sparkle to her eyes when, flaunting her knowledge that I had been appointed a teaching fellow for the coming academic year, she would introduce me as "the Harvard professor who is mowing our lawn this summer." She outraged her own retired governess by sitting in the front seat to chat with me during some of our afternoon drives and on every morning of our long trip at the end of the summer. She often invited Pat to join us on our afternoon drives to parks or historic sites. Knowing that Pat's father was a Presbyterian minister, she always invited her to ride to church with us on Sunday morning and to sit next to her during the service. And when some of my friends from Harvard camped in our little cottage for the weekend, she insisted that they join us for the Sunday morning service.

She even appreciated a breach of decorum committed involuntarily in the church by one of our guests. During the summer the church invited ministers of several Protestant denominations to serve as guest preachers, and the visiting preacher on the day of my guest's indiscretion was described in the church bulletin as "the most decorated chaplain of World War II." We arrived early, as Mrs. Curtis always did, and we were therefore settled in her pew before the ministers had taken their places in the chancel. Whether or not the visiting preacher was the most decorated chaplain of the Second World War, he was certainly the most decorated preacher any of us had ever seen in Episcopal vestments. He wore a white robe and stole. Gleaming against the white background on his breast were four or five rows of battle ribbons. Now our two guests had also done hazardous duty, one in the navy and the other in the army air corps, and they were amazed by the sight of those ribbons. Larry Holland, the naval veteran, had developed a wheezing, gasping laugh. As the visiting preacher came into view, Larry's laugh and his wheezing exclamation, "I don't believe it!," whistled through the church.

The year was 1948, the summer of Elizabeth Bentley's testimony that she had been a courier for Communist spies in the federal government, the summer of Whittaker Chambers's accusations against Alger Hiss, the summer of Henry Wallace's campaign against Harry Truman's Cold War presidency, the summer in which Republicans felt confident of winning the presidential election for the first time in twenty years. "David," Mrs. Curtis had said to me one morning as we set out on a four-hour trip, "do you ever have any fears that Dewey won't win?" The glares directed at our indecorous young guest by the people around us in the church were reinforced by the former chaplain's flagrantly political sermon. "We don't need all these material comforts, all these gadgets, that the workingman seeks to acquire," said the preacher to his congregation of millionaires. He deplored the quest for complete security. He praised the Taft-Hartley Act as a necessary curb on Big Labor, and he called Henry Wallace "that long-eared jackass."

Mrs. Curtis was indignant, not at Larry Holland, but at the preacher. "I see no place for that kind of language in a Christian church," she said. "Henry Wallace may be gullible, but I do think he is an *honest* fool, and"—with her naughty smile—"he was once a good Republican." When Larry apologized for his own outburst, which he described as involuntary, Mrs. Curtis reassured him. "Of course it was! I'm sure that priest is a brave man, for I've never seen so many ribbons on one man, but I must confess that this is the first time I have ever seen even one on a minister's stole."

My status, then, was that of a resident tutor, jester, companion, as well as the less ambiguous rank of my stated duties. Pat called me a literary conversationalist in waiting. The liveried chauffeurs of Watch Hill knew about these Harvard students who worked for Mrs. Curtis every summer—we would read books while waiting outside the large cocktail and dinner parties during the season—and so they generally ignored me. I not only wore my ordinary clothes (usually a sport shirt, sometimes a jacket and tie) when driving but also sometimes entered my employer's house through the front door rather than the kitchen. When Mrs. Curtis learned that I had worked as a playground instructor and baseball coach in Boston's Park Department throughout the summer of 1947, she drafted me to play tennis with her seventeen-year-old grandson and to coach his ten-year-old brother, who showed promise as a catcher, in baseball. One Sunday I was even called on to be Mrs. Lombard's partner in a round-robin tennis tournament at her club, because her husband was playing in a golf tournament that afternoon.

The complexity of my status gave Pat and me little trouble, for it was easy to see that, unless otherwise instructed, I had access to the house only through Bessie's kitchen, where I also received most of my orders, and that the lawns of the two houses had to be mowed regularly (without a power mower), the roses and shrubs pruned and weeded, the groceries picked up in Westerly when Bessie ordered them. Pat and I could swim whenever we wished in the little cove just behind Mrs. Curtis's house, but we usually did not venture in when we looked down from the lawn late in the morning and saw two white heads bobbing there, the toes of four white swimming slippers pointing up as Mrs. Curtis and Bessie planned the next day's meals. Bessie's brogue and Mrs. Curtis's melodious high and low notes would float up to us, naming in their contrasting accents the vegetables and sauces and desserts of haute cuisine. Bessie knew her place even when she was swimming beside Mrs. Curtis; I knew mine when Mrs. Curtis sat beside me on the front seat of her car or (as she did once) at her friend's dinner table.

Of course Pat and I knew that our easy acceptance of the situation owed as much to our certainty that we would be there only a few months as it owed to my employer's confidence and generosity. Even in those days of our early twenties, we had some sense of the implicit condescension in our relationship to the servants and to the masters. In return for some hard work—Pat helped me in the garden and occasionally hired out as kitchen help for large private parties—we had a cottage on a cool peninsula during a very hot summer. In return for the embarrassments in our anomalous status, we had not only the privilege of entertaining our friends as house guests but also the educational experience and the pleasure of coming to know something about this world of masters and servants, and even to make some friends in it. I did not see so clearly then as I do now that if Mrs. Curtis was using us, we were also using her. As I was her "Harvard professor," whose candidacy for a degree in the History of American Sieve-ill-eye-zation could make her eyes light up with both patriotism and a little mockery, so she was my aristocrat, whom I teased a little by taking full advantage of her encouragement to tell her what I really thought about political issues, and about whose strange new world I knew even then that I would one day want to write. Pat and I knew, too, that whatever pain we felt or complications we caused in the Curtis and Lombard households would not require any adjustments in our lives after I had delivered Mrs. Curtis to her apartment on East 69th Street at Lexington Avenue at the end of our visit to Williamstown, Massachusetts, in mid-September.

Yet I was surprised and offended when Mrs. Lombard came to

me one day in early July to ask me to spend less time talking to her butler. "Surely you see, David, that your position is different from Jerry's," she said. "Your duties occasionally require you to join Mother's guests in the living room, and if you associate too casually with Jerry, who is only now learning the nuances of our way, he may be misled into thinking he ought to have the same privileges in our house."

Jerry, of course, had brought from the Nova Scotia mines a much stronger sense of class than most Americans will ever acquire. I did not tell Mrs. Lombard about the conversation in which Jerry had already commented on my mobility. "Jesus," he had sworn, "you pass through those walls as easily as if you were a ghost!" He and I had had two or three good discussions of academic status in the United States. He had especially enjoyed my quotation of President Lowell's famous decree that an education in the undergraduate houses at Harvard must make scholars out of gentlemen and gentlemen out of scholars. Since the butler's family would be on vacation for two weeks while the Lombards were off sailing a rented yacht, it was easy for me to concede to Mrs. Lombard that, although I couldn't simply drop Jerry, I would try, after his return from vacation, to drop in a little less often. But I insisted that I thought he did see the difference between his position and mine. I did not ask her what evidence she had to the contrary, and she volunteered none.

The difference between the two Curtis generations, I now believe, was partly attributable to age and partly to character. It was inconceivable that such a problem could have arisen in Mrs. Curtis's household. The servants may have resented Mrs. Curtis's reception of her Harvard students, but they would have claimed no such liberties for themselves, and she herself would never have objected to our spending as much free time as we wished in conversations with Bessie or Mary.

Despite our mobility and our delight in Bessie, Mrs. Curtis, and Jamie Lombard, the ten-year-old grandson who did *not* play baseball and who hated being shipped off every morning to take tennis and swimming lessons at the yacht club, Pat and I did suffer our own little difficulties with the prevailing manners of Watch Hill's summer colony. Pat had a harrowing time presiding over a birthday luncheon for nine-year-old boys at the home of the celebrant's grandmother, who had to attend a party at a friend's house that day. Pat said she felt like a visiting teacher in a rich elementary school. The boys threw chunks of lobster at one another, and then began a water fight with the contents of the finger bowls that were brought in with dessert. More distressing than the party itself was the series of implicitly suspicious telephone calls from the absentee grandmother during the next several days, asking whether Pat had noticed a gold necklace, which now could not be found. When the necklace turned up in a drawer that for some reason had not been searched, the apology to my dear wife, the suffering suspect, was perfunctory. Mrs. Curtis was warmly indignant.

In my own encounter with finger bowls, Mrs. Curtis was equally supportive. Perhaps because I had spent only one semester in Lowell House before joining the army air force, President Lowell's university had not yet completed my transformation into a gentleman. Mrs. Curtis was invited to dinner in Stonington at the home of the retired president of Connecticut College for Women, and she arranged for me to be invited as well, presumably on the ground that a former college president ought to be interested in a young Harvard "professor" who was studying American civilization.

It was a very small party. I don't remember feeling troubled by the age of the guests, all of whom were over seventy, or by the formal dress of the one other man at the table. I was so busy answering questions about American civilization, and observing which fork, spoon, and knife Mrs. Curtis used, that I had little time to notice my nervousness. When the finger bowls were brought to the table, I observed that a mint leaf was floating in each bowl. When she removed her leaf, I removed mine, and when she began to pat hers gently by folding her napkin over it I patted mine in the same way. She was talking with her usual animation at the time, and failed to notice my imitative gestures. To my horror, then, she tucked the fragrant leaf into the bosom of her gown.

I continued lamely to pat my leaf, and my loyal friend and employer insisted on the way home that neither she nor anyone else at the table had seen any oddity in my mimicry. "Why *shouldn't* you pat the leaf and enjoy its fragrance?" she asked me. She would hear nothing of any faux pas, and she ended the discussion by insisting on an axiom that I had read in Edith Wharton: Don't apologize, and never explain. I told her that in my family the opposite axiom ruled: "Often apologize, always explain," and the worst of my embarrassment seemed to dissolve in our mutual laughter.

She was equally charming and supportive when I had to consult her about a much more unpleasant encounter in Watch Hill. I saw in the local newspaper an advertisement for a small apartment in the town, near the public beach and the shops, at a price my parents could afford. Hoping to persuade them to spend their vacation near us, I telephoned the agent to inquire about renting the place for them for a week or two. "Do you mind," the agent said coolly, "if I ask about their religion?"

Since I hadn't yet given him my name, I didn't learn whether the implicit proscription excluded only Jews or Catholics as well. I told him that I certainly did mind, and I went directly to Mrs. Curtis.

Now in 1948 as in 1989 one assumed that membership in the country club or yacht club in a place like Watch Hill was tacitly closed to Jews. I despised such a social system, but I could live in it as a temporary employee and an observer. I could even agree to play in the mixed doubles tournament as part of my job. I had been painfully amused once when a five-year-old granddaughter of Mrs. Curtis, on being told that a park we passed was a public park, said, "Oh, that's where the colored people go." And I had noticed that the Olympia, an ice-cream parlor and café in town, was universally known as "the Greek's." What shocked me in my telephone conversation was not only the casually bigoted rejection of my parents, but also the discovery that a commercially advertised, inexpensive property in the public part of town could be governed by such benighted rules. By the time I had arranged an interview with Mrs. Curtis, I had resolved to explain my feelings to her and to tell her that, although I had assumed the signature on my first letter had identified my religious background, I would leave at once if these quaint rules applied to chauffeur-gardeners and literary conversationalists in waiting.

She heard me out with sympathetic exclamations. "Oh, dear!" she said when I had finished. "It's a shame. We must *do* something about finding a suitable place for your parents to stay." When I assured her that my parents wouldn't now think of coming even if I would consider inviting them, she returned to the subject of Watch Hill. "Of *course* I recognized your name in your first letter, and soon afterward I had my chauffeur stop when we passed a store named Levin's in Manhattan. All the clerks there looked Jewish, so that settled that." She waved off my effort to comment on the strange logic and dubious ethics of that anecdote. "It didn't make the slightest difference to me; I had already hired you. But in the company I keep, especially at Tuxedo Park and here in Watch Hill, it was only prudent to be prepared." Then she told me about the great battle over the residency of David Lawrence, a conservative political columnist for the New York *Herald Tribune,* who she said was a well-known Jewish convert to Episcopal Christianity. By marrying an Episcopalian woman who spent her summers in Watch Hill, Lawrence had unwittingly provoked a debate over his eligibility to live in Watch Hill with her, and Mrs. Curtis had supported him. She persuaded me that she genuinely deplored arbitrary exclusions of this kind even while she spent much of her time in the social world that they (and what she considered affirmative selections) defined. She was what she was. There was no point in my trying to change her.

I saw the affirmative side of her personal code again in her families' reactions that summer to the accusations against Alger Hiss and a man named Ivan Stokes, neither of whom I had heard of before. The strong assumption was that these political opponents were decent men and that the tactics used against them were unacceptable, even in the year of a presidential election. Three years later, when she invited Pat and me to visit her for a weekend in Watch Hill, Mrs. Curtis vigorously defended Dean Acheson against the accusations of one of her other young guests. She accepted the jury's verdict of Hiss's guilt, she said, but she insisted that Acheson's refusal to turn his back on his old friend had been perfectly proper.

The summer passed agreeably, then, and much of it delightfully, as Pat and I grew fond of our elderly new friend. For two weeks we took care of the Lombards' empty house and their two dogs, mixing great chunks of garlic in with the meat on the mistaken belief, in those days before tick collars, that ticks find garlic repellent. (We found the bloated ticks and the dogs' breath and wind repellent.) We took Mrs. Curtis and one of her guests to Old Mystic, and they went happily through the whaling ship with us. We ourselves were permitted to have what one of the Curtis grandchildren called masses of guests, and at the end of the summer Mrs. Curtis and I drove to Williamstown for her annual ten days' visit with an old friend.

Our hosts in Williamstown were a retired Huguenot minister and his wife, whose name was something like Van Brundt. I was given a room in a tourist home across the street from the Van Brundts' house. As a favor to Mrs. Van Brundt, Mrs. Curtis was persuaded to accept an invitation to tea from a Mrs. Treadway, a middle-aged woman whose husband was proprietor of several Treadway inns. Mrs. Curtis soon came out to summon me because the conversation had turned to literature, and I could see as soon as I entered the room that Mrs. Treadway was eager to please the grand old lady. The three women talked about the obscure meaning in much modern literature, and of course they deplored the growing attention to sex and other subjects they considered unpleasant or improper. Mrs. Treadway said that her daughter had given her a copy of Truman Capote's *Other Voices, Other Rooms* as a birthday present, and she confessed that she could not understand what it was about. Then she asked me if I knew.

When I uttered the word *homosexual,* I ruined Mrs. Treadway's day. She herself did not blanch or complain, but my own Mrs. Curtis, who had allowed me every freedom of opinion and discussion, could not bear to hear that word uttered in polite company, not even when it was used descriptively in answer to a question that made it necessary. "Filth!" she exclaimed, shuddering and rattling her teacup. "That is why I gave up my subscription to *Harper's;* they printed an article about sex psychology in the Christmas issue!" She made a perfunctory excuse for having to leave after a *lovely* tea, and ten minutes later we were walking to the car. I did not apologize or explain.

At the Treadways' I saw Mrs. Curtis's composure shaken, but not her social confidence; in that house she was evidently the person of superior status. The ambiguous incident that I mentioned at the beginning of this little memoir occurred the next day, when we called on Mrs. Prentiss, the daughter of John D. Rockefeller, at Mount Hope. I had been told to wear my sport jacket and a necktie for this visit. When we arrived at the top of the mountain, I was sent to the imposing front door with the calling cards of Mrs. Curtis and her hostess, only to learn that Mrs. Prentiss had gone out for a drive. I returned to the shiny black Buick, the 1946 sedan that looked like a fat beetle, and we started down the long, sinuous drive. On one of the curves, banked to our right as we descended, we encountered an open Pierce Arrow touring sedan carrying, behind the chauffeur, a tiny old woman and three gentlemen wearing dark suits and homburgs.

Mrs. Van Brundt called out, "Stop, David!," and I stopped, not too abruptly, so that, listing about ten degrees to starboard, we were just past being abreast of the Pierce Arrow, which had also stopped.

No sooner had I applied the brakes, however, than Mrs. Curtis commanded me to drive on. Both cars moved a few feet as I responded to that command and the Prentiss chauffeur reacted.

But Mrs. Van Brundt cried immediately, "Oh, Cornelia, it's all right; I'm sure they'll be glad to see us." I stopped then, and so did the other car.

"Drive on at *once,* David!" came my stern command from Mrs. Curtis. In the mirror I saw her rebuke Mrs. Van Brundt with a quick glance even as she spoke to me, and then she smiled a farewell to the group who were listing to port above and behind us. The gentlemen in that car, obeying no signal that I could hear, lifted their hats in unison as both cars drove away.

Now it may be that Mrs. Curtis was flustered by the grandeur of the Rockefellers, but I believe she was merely enforcing two social principles: It was *her* car and driver to command, not her hostess's; and while it was all right to go calling at the proper hour, it was not acceptable to call on people who were just arriving. Within a minute or two the ladies in the back seat were as cordial to each other as ever, and the next day, when they were invited to a musicale at Mount Hope, Mrs. Curtis did not hesitate to telephone Mrs. Prentiss and ask that I be allowed to attend, on the pretense that I was a devoted student of organ music. That flagrant fiction Mrs. Curtis defended against my protest by reminding me, with zany logic, that my brother was a pianist.

As we entered the great hall on the day of the musicale, Mrs. Prentiss greeted us cordially. She was prepared for my status if not for my name. She led me across the hall as she spoke. "So nice to see you, Mr. Ludden. Now you come right over to the keyboard so that you can watch every detail of Arthur Borden's technique; I've asked him to tell you as much as he can about our organ and to answer your questions." Before I had time to resist, she had introduced me to Mr. Borden and gone back to the foyer to welcome the dozens of arriving guests.

While the guests were arriving, Mr. Borden was playing Strauss waltzes. "You'll never see another organ like this in a private home," he said gloomily, talking over his shoulder as he rocked back and forth and played on; "they're taxing them out of existence. You know what they ought to do with that little haberdasher in the White House? They should take him and his piano and his singing daughter and his cronies, and ship them all back to Independence, Missouri, where he can play the 'Missouri Waltz' for the rest of his life. And in less than two months that's exactly what the American people are going to do."

Irritating as this monologue might have been in another context, it seemed to me hilariously welcome here, for it spared me the embarrassment of revealing my total ignorance concerning the construction of organs and the techniques of playing them. The monologue ended when the guests were all seated, and I gratefully retreated to the folding chair that Mrs. Curtis had saved for me. I did know enough to enjoy the sound of that fine instrument and the high quality of the organist's performance. Mrs. Prentiss herself played two short pieces on a new electronic instrument called the novichord, and then, after a splendid finale by Mr. Borden, the party was over.

We rode back to Williamstown in almost complete silence. Mrs. Curtis did ask me how I liked the sound of the organ, and whether I had learned anything from Mr. Borden. "He helped me to understand how the instrument works," I lied, "and I thought he played splendidly. By the way, do they never serve refreshments at such a party?"

"I too was surprised," Mrs. Curtis said. "David, how would you like to have an ice-cream soda? I think we deserve a reward for our patience. Having heard the novichord and descended to the soda fountain in Williamstown, we shall have gone from the ridiculous to the sublime."

So the three of us went to the drugstore for our ice-cream sodas, and in one of my last and fondest memories of Mrs. Curtis I am sitting between her and Mrs. Van Brundt on a stool at the soda fountain. An elegant hat shades Mrs. Curtis's face under the artificial light as she leans over the glass to drink through the straw. In my uncertain memory her legs are not quite long enough to reach the foot rest, and as her blue eyes shine happily I see the delight of the child surviving in the seventy-five-year-old woman.

We did see her several times in the next few years. She persuaded me to drive her from Watch Hill to Williamstown again when my successor could not make the trip at the end of the following summer, and we visited her at the Lombards' house in Dedham, again in Watch Hill, and the last time in her own apartment in Manhattan. Even after we had moved to California, she always acknowledged promptly and with some relevant comment the offprints of articles that I sent her, and in her late middle eighties she sent me a lovely note about my first book. For me she made the affirmative side of Edith Wharton's social world credible. In personal loyalty, civility, compassion, and considerateness, she exemplified the best values of her class. And in her response to me and my young friends she became one of several septuagenarians who, though they could not be called intellectuals, continued to grow mentally by maintaining a lively interest in the new ideas and experience of the young.

WALLACE STEGNER

NAMES AND PLACES

Wallace Stegner's name had special meaning for me a decade before it helped to set the direction of my professional life. Stegner was celebrated as a teacher of composition during my freshman year at Harvard, 1941–42. My roommate, who was assigned to his class, continued to praise him months after our graded and revised themes—which we were not allowed to keep until they were returned to us in the last week of our senior year—had been tied neatly into folded packets and stored away somewhere in Warren House. Although *The Big Rock Candy Mountain* had not yet appeared, Stegner had already published several volumes of fiction. He was one of the brightest young stars in a constellation that included Mark Schorer, Delmore Schwartz, and Albert J. Guerard.

Stegner, Guerard, and Schorer (as well as Harry Levin, Perry Miller, H. M. Jones, F. O. Matthiessen, Frederick Merk, A. M. Schlesinger, and Stegner's friend Bernard DeVoto) were all midwesterners or westerners. Even in those early days, when President Conant had only recently established the National Scholarships to recruit students from outside New England, Harvard had attracted able minds from the heartland and the West. In the tradition of William Dean Howells, Mark Twain, and Josiah Royce, many of these writers and scholars had stayed on the East Coast. DeVoto remained bitter about Harvard's refusal to promote him to a permanent professorship but stayed in the neighborhood, and when I knew Mark Schorer in California in the 1950s and 1960s I often had the impression that he would have liked to return to the East from Berkeley.

By the time Stegner's name came to affect my own life, however, both he and the name were identified with Stanford, with California, and with the West. True, his publishers were in Boston and then New York; he maintained a summer house in Greensboro, Vermont; his commissioned assignments, his literary success, and his political curiosity took him to Europe and the Middle East. But for more than forty years he has firmly, and sometimes defiantly, identified himself as a westerner. When first told to invoke his name, I was told that he did not regard himself as an exile in California, and I remembered that admonition years later when Stegner defined the true surviving West as "the last of the sticks—the subregions between the ninety-eighth meridian and the Sierra-Cascades, where patterns of local habit and belief have developed in some isolation."*

My emphasis on his *name's* effect on my life needs some explanation. In 1951–52, when I first sought a full-time academic post, neither Harvard's name on my return address nor my own at the end of the letter of application would have elicited a reply from Stanford or any comparable university. The academic marketplace had just begun to be a little more open than in the 1930s. No longer was a candidate told, as one of my predecessors at Harvard had been advised, to "play the blushing bride." In 1951 a candidate could send out a few unsolicited letters without seeming presumptuous, but only at the suggestion of a well-known adviser, and preferably by addressing the letter to one of the adviser's friends. The relatively open market of the 1970s and 1980s, with nationally published "job lists" and scores of applications for every position, had hardly been dreamed of. Most universities still recruited by discreetly asking a few department chairmen or eminent professors to nominate a graduate student (as Perry Miller had tapped

*Wallace Stegner, "Born a Square: The Westerner's Dilemma," *Atlantic* 213, no. 1 (January 1964): 48.

me for the post at Bennington). Theodore Morrison, director of Harvard's freshman-English program, wrote to Wallace Stegner about me, and my letter to the Stanford chairman relied on the names and the mutual trust of Morrison, who had supervised my teaching, and Stegner, who had never seen me.

In that changing marketplace, names occasionally figured in an even narrower way at the other end of the scale. Vestiges of the old system still survive, in letters or telephone calls asking us to nominate one or two of our best students in a designated field. But no student in the 1980s could be told by his chairman, as Kenneth Murdock told me in December 1951, that a request for nominees to teach at Duke University had plainly said no Jew would be considered. Murdock's pointed way of defying the restriction, he told me, was to send my unacceptable name along with two that were not what we now call ethnic—and then to warn me to expect no word from Duke.

Even today, thirty-seven years after I joined the Stanford faculty, I have no way of knowing whether Morrison's referral through Stegner tacitly certified the social acceptability of this Jewish candidate. Nor did I know then that as late as 1924 David Starr Jordan, Stanford's revered former president, had deplored the immigration of "the Irish, the Greeks, the South Italians and the Polish Jews" because they included "elements permanently deficient in the best traits we can hope for in America."* I *can* testify that Stanford welcomed me warmly, that the English department recruited several other Jews during my years at Stanford, and that I never heard so much as a whisper of anti-Semitism in the department—though I did learn years later that several history professors had openly objected to appointing any Jew as a colleague.

Such exclusions touched my very fortunate life only rarely. It was for my generation that they were virtually erased. Or perhaps

*Quoted by Marcia Graham Synnott, "Anti-Semitism and American Universities," in *Anti-Semitism in American History*, ed. David Gerber (Champaign: University of Illinois Press, 1986), p. 264.

the new floods of Jews and other outsiders simply washed out the restrictive lines as colleges and universities expanded in the decades after World War II. As Harvard freshmen all my Jewish classmates and I had been assigned Jewish roommates before we arrived, but I saw no reason to believe rumors of unofficial quotas until a book about Ivy League restrictions (1979) proved that they had been both widespread and precise.* Both before and after the war, everyone knew that many medical schools strictly limited the number of Jews admitted, and when the Stanford Medical School moved from San Francisco to Stanford in the late 1950s, some of us savored as delicious irony the influx of Jewish families—with intense official publicity for the Nobel laureates Joshua Lederberg and Arthur Kornberg—to faculty housing on the campus.

As late as 1970, the names of Kornberg and Lederberg turned up in a different way. I served as chairman of the university's commitee on graduate study at a time when William Shockley, himself a Nobel laureate in applied physics, asked the dean of the Graduate Division to sponsor Shockley's proposed course on heredity and intelligence. Although Cyril Burtt's bogus evidence on identical twins had not yet been proven fraudulent, Shockley's inferences from Burtt's study and others had long been notorious. Every few months, it seemed, the Palo Alto *Times* or one of the metropolitan dailies would run a feature article on Shockley's claim that liberal scientists were trying to silence him for fear of having to face evidence of Afro-Americans' allegedly inferior intelligence. Shockley's campaign to persuade the National Academy of Sciences to sponsor such a study had provoked a dozen or so geneticists at Stanford to publish an open letter denouncing the genetic premises of his argument. When I alluded to their letter in a discussion of Shockley's proposed course, an astronomer argued *ad nomina:* "Look at those signatures," he said, "Leder-

*See Marcia Graham Synnott, *The Half-Opened Door: Discrimination and Admissions at Harvard, Yale, and Princeton, 1900–1970* (Westport: Greenwood Press, 1979), p. 112.

berg, Kornberg, and the rest. Surely you don't expect those ethnics to approve a study of racial characteristics!"

Of course other Jewish names—Felix Bloch, Leonard Schiff, Marvin Chodorow, Herman Chernoff, and half a dozen more—figured prominently in the natural sciences and mathematics when I arrived, but there were none in English or history, and so few Jewish residents of the area that no synagogue or temple existed in Palo Alto, Menlo Park, Mountain View, or Los Altos. Stanford students had neither a chapter of Hillel nor any Jewish fraternities.

Mrs. Leland Stanford's opposition to sectarianism made this situation seem less anomalous than it would now. Mrs. Stanford had insisted long ago that the church at the center of the Inner Quad be nondenominational, and as late as the 1950s no churches at all had representatives at Stanford. Lutherans and other Protestants who wished to consult a chaplain of their own persuasion had to find these counselors in off-campus centers established by the denominations. Roman Catholic students could worship at the Newman Center in Palo Alto, but in those days Catholic priests were not invited—or could not accept invitations—to take a turn among the various Protestant ministers and the Reform rabbi as guest preacher on Sunday morning at the Stanford Memorial Church.

Some of the discomfort that a Jewish student or professor might experience in the 1950s could be attributed to the ambience of conformity rather than to anti-Semitism alone. Several fraternities on campus excluded undergraduates of Jewish, Asian, or African descent. For a time more Africans than Afro-Americans were enrolled. Female students had to wear "quad clothes"—dresses or skirts; no jeans, slacks, or shorts—in the academic area, but male undergraduates sometimes came to class barefoot and wearing shorts. Men's folklore celebrated the traditional Ratio, which decreed that enrollment would include 2.8 undergraduate men for every woman.

All those restrictions disappeared before the end of my nineteen years on the Stanford faculty. The winds of freedom, proudly invoked in Stanford's motto, did blow steadily, if gently, through that ambience, making the odor of discrimination somewhat less pervasive. Even in the 1950s and early 1960s it was clear that if quotas really did exclude qualified Jewish students, some Jewish alumni and alumnae not only loved the university enough to give and solicit funds, but also served on the board of trustees or had their names attached permanently to important buildings.

What I knew about Wallace Stegner's name as I drove west in September 1952 had no ethnic content. Not until years later, as a colleague and friend who had read virtually all of his work, did I begin to appreciate the complex meanings of a Scandinavian background in Salt Lake City or East End, Saskatchewan. As I look back through the layers of subsequent knowledge and experience, however, I cannot avoid seeing my first transcontinental drive with full knowledge that Stegner despised Bernard Malamud's *A New Life,* the novel about "S. Levin, formerly a drunkard." Much of the hilarity in that flawed, farcical *roman à clef* depends on an urban easterner's clumsy response not only to the vast spaces and immense trees of Oregon, but also to the private automobile, the vehicle that is useless in Manhattan yet essential to the rudimentary civilization of the West. By the time *A New Life* was published in 1961, I was already a committed Californian, well enough acquainted with eastern condescension to appreciate Stegner's indignation. Perhaps I could take more delight than Stegner found in Malamud's ridicule of S. Levin's own eastern provincialism, but I saw that much of Malamud's humor addresses a reader who must be an outsider looking down on crude western mores.

As Pat and I set out on our own new life in 1952, however, I was a much more experienced chauffeur than Malamud's S. Levin, and I had already seen much of the West. For nearly two of my three years in the army air force, I had lived in Texas and New Mexico. At Kirtland Field near Albuquerque, free of the western farmer's anxiety about drought—free too of his need to cope with the danger in the wide open spaces—I had learned to love the dry landscape, the green refuge in the Pecos River canyon, the cool summer nights, the open skies, the sense of unlimited distances. In training missions I had navigated our B-29 to a rendezvous at dawn over the Grand Canyon, and then on a fifteen-hour flight, shooting sun lines by day and fixes on stars at night, all the way to Los Angeles, up the coast to Portland, and back. At another dawn, July 16, 1945, the open sky had lighted up so brilliantly behind us (as we pulled our propellers through to clear the cylinders before boarding) that all eleven crewmen fell to the ground, startled by the first atomic fireball when it burst near Alamogordo, 140 miles away.

Some of those images of space returned to me as I drove toward Stegner's West in our three-year-old Chevrolet. I had often seen the great wall of the Rockies from the air and had felt the exhilaration of living nearly a mile above sea level in New Mexico, but not until my Chevy pulled a U-Haul trailer across Kansas and Colorado—with the car's rear end down low and both the temperature gauge and the headlights pointing upward—did I feel the uphill drag that must have oppressed oxen and the emigrants plodding toward the Continental Divide a hundred years before us. I thought of scenes from Stegner's *The Big Rock Candy Mountain* not only when we cooked our supper beside the Great Salt Lake, but also one evening a few days earlier, when our cocker spaniel suddenly stiffened and pointed her nose into the wind as we picnicked on a bleak plateau near Rock Springs, Wyoming. The big sky was so clear and the land so empty that we couldn't tell whether the six antelope off there in the dusk were one mile away or five.

Instruction in western perspective came at close range, too. My first jackrabbit, transfixed by my headlights, seemed to stand four feet tall when it loomed in the road, somewhere between Elko and Winnemucca, Nevada. I did resist the impulse to brake, but without thinking about the trailer I swerved. We missed the rabbit and bounced down the highway for several hundred feet, first on the three right wheels and then on the three left. Immediately, before flattened carcasses on the road taught me on the next day that rabbits were not so big as they looked at night, I learned that I must hold the wheel steady even if that meant running over the next rabbit standing in our way. Bleeding heart that I am, I acknowledged a guilty communion with the ranchers in Frank Norris's *The Octopus,* who form a line across the wheat fields, frighten hundreds of jackrabbits into a corral, and then trample and club them to death.

Not until ten years later, when Stegner published *Wolf Willow,* would I learn that as a small boy helping his father grow wheat across the border in Saskatchewan, Stegner had become expert in killing rodents: "we knew to the slightest kick and reflex the gophers' way of dying: knew how the eyes popped out blue as marbles when we clubbed a trapped gopher with a stake, knew how a gopher shot in the behind just as he dove into his hole would sometimes back right out again with ridiculous promptness and die in the open."* But before I headed west in 1952, Stegner, an incomparably better craftsman than Norris, had already taught me in *The Preacher and the Slave* (1950—reissued nineteen years later as *Joe Hill*) complex truths about farm labor in California and about history in fiction. I was better prepared for agribusiness, for the slow trucks dragging incredible loads of tomatoes through the Niles Canyon in double trailers, than for the tiny quarter-acre boxes, rigidly defined by wooden fences six feet high, into which inhabitants were dividing the great western spaces. Nothing in the Bay Area surprised me more than this cramping—not the brown hills that turned green in December, or the clouds of fog that told me to carry an umbrella and raincoat every morning in late September and then evaporated before noon to leave me feeling foolish in the brilliant sunlight.

Attaching Stegner's name to the region was my way of acknowledging his literary skill and my fortuitous association with him. Before I actually met him, I learned one other startling fact about

*Wallace Stegner, *Wolf Willow: A History, A Story, and A Memory of the Last Plains Frontier* (New York: Viking, 1962), p. 275.

the local significance of his name. A wealthy donor, brother of the retired executive head of the Stanford English department, had endowed fellowships for young writers of poetry and fiction. He had named them for Wallace Stegner and had left Stegner free to take them along if he should ever leave Stanford for another university. Before encountering Stegner in person, I was deeply impressed by the literary achievement and the personal address of a writer who in his early forties had already been honored by a group of fellowships bearing his name.

2

Reality matched expectation, but biography brought more surprises. Whereas I mistakenly expected Yvor Winters to look like an abstemious curmudgeon, everything I had heard about Stegner prepared me for an All-American gentleman, naturally at ease and winning in personality. Everyone spoke affectionately of him, and here he was, a handsome, athletic-looking man with hooded eyes like John Wayne's and a musical baritone voice. He had obviously cultivated his talent for metaphors, not only in writing but in conversation. His speech, like the lines I have quoted about gophers, often showed you that he observed details acutely and that he remembered them. His disarmingly youthful delivery and the aptness of his choices made this artful speech seem as natural as the poems of his old friend Robert Frost or the deceptively simple monologues of Mark Twain. Sometimes the analogue was as recondite as the description of the gophers; often too the effect depended on a succinct appeal to more nearly universal experience. When someone asked him what he thought of Rachel Carson's exposé of the dangers of insecticides, Stegner responded promptly: "From now on I'll stamp my ants."

The qualities that made Stegner exemplary for me were discipline and versatility. I never learned to follow his strict routine during the academic year—writing for at least a couple of hours every morning and teaching in the afternoon. When I taught after noon I needed all the morning hours to prepare and review for my classes. Nor did I discover whatever secret, beyond superior intelligence and articulateness, enabled Stegner to remain a first-class, universally respected teacher while adhering to his routine, year after year. My wonder and the secret persisted down through 1987, when Stegner (at seventy-eight) published a novel whose young protagonist, unquestionably a very hard worker, manages to continue writing even after he has learned that he must immediately teach a new course in world literature.

Stegner's versatility was even more impressive. In this colleague the reconciling that I had admired in F. O. Matthiessen's history and literature program seemed to be given a personal expression, and to be intensified and extended. Here was a writer of stories and novels who also distinguished himself as a scholarly biographer and historian. Among his good friends were the physicist Leonard Schiff and the anthropologist Felix Keesing, and Stegner's research into the life of Major John Wesley Powell gave him the geological metaphor that would serve as the title for his best novel, *Angle of Repose* ("the slope at which rocks cease to roll"). In the heady days when the Democratic party was just beginning to revive in California, after right-wing Republicans had sewn up the governorship and the United States Senate seat by winning the Democratic primaries in 1952, Stegner (with our colleague the historian H. Stuart Hughes) moved easily among the political leaders and major financial contributors in northern California. He introduced Adlai Stevenson at a rally during the presidential campaign of 1952. He studied and wrote about small democratic communities in Denmark, Vermont, and Norway. He became a trusted consultant on national issues of conservation, and one of the first fellows at the new Center for Advanced Study in the Behavioral Sciences, and for a time a leader in the American Civil Liberties Union. At Stanford, meanwhile, he continued to teach popular courses on the rise of realism and the development of the short story as well as his seminars in fiction writing and twentieth-century fiction, and to direct the graduate and undergraduate programs in creative writing.

Besides teaching me some salutary humility, the prodigies of scholarship that I had observed at Harvard had prepared me to live without astonishment in a community of extraordinary achievers. What set Wallace Stegner's versatility apart was the easy grace with which he seemed to manage his demanding activities. It was not effortless, but natural; one saw no sign of strain. Until I read the astonishing words in *Wolf Willow* in 1962, I would not have believed that as a boy this man had been "skinny and small," a "crybaby" who "always had a runny nose" and whose father had ridiculed him as a "mama's boy" (p. 130). Speaking to a small audience for the ACLU; introducing Robert Frost and Frank O'Connor at readings that filled Memorial Auditorium; receiving scores of colleagues and students at his redwood house in the hills between Stanford and the coastal range, or moving among hundreds of guests at a fund-raising reception in the Edward Heller mansion in Atherton; negotiating for Stanford's acquisition of the DeVoto papers; responding to aggressively unorthodox graduate students in creative writing, and to an insulting crank who berated him during the question period after a public lecture in the student union—Stegner expressed in all these situations the same graceful mastery.

Understated as it was, this quality differed from Robert Frost's rustic platform manner. Homely, practical examples abounded in Stegner's speech, an informal, boyish directness that had some of the quality (though with more maturity, and without the "aw shucks!") seen in the personae of James Stewart or Henry Fonda. If both Stegner's and Frost's personae owed something to the tradition of Ben Franklin, Abe Lincoln, Mark Twain, and Will Rogers, Stegner did not invoke the cracker barrel. I did hear him (as I had heard Perry Miller, S. E. Morison, and Yvor Winters) say that he preferred to be known as a writer rather than as a professor, and he would sometimes use the diminutive (Jimmy Baldwin, Benny DeVoto) in speaking of fellow writers, but I never saw him stoop to the crowd-pleasing tricks with which Frost had offended some of our colleagues. I believe Frost's act *was* more complicated than it seemed: both he and most of his audience knew he was playing a role when he lampooned over-inventive interpreters of "Stopping by Woods on a Snowy Evening." ("A footnote," Frost said, "is too late.") Yet for all his admiration of Frost, Stegner did not endorse the command that we heard Frost issue to hundreds of undergraduates the last time Frost "said" his poems at Stanford: "Never take a course in poetry." In speech and in much of Stegner's writing—as in the early pages of *The Uneasy Chair,* Stegner's biography of DeVoto—the voice was informal but not folksy. He did not need to pretend that literature requires no study. Even when he addressed a large audience, he could establish familiarity without condescending.

What I have called grace or natural ease implies also a sense of moral and intellectual balance. I perceived that balance in Stegner even when I mistakenly believed he had always possessed it as a natural gift. Learning that a crybaby had acquired it through study and discipline, that he had earned his ease, made its moral significance all the more impressive. His agile versatility seemed to declare that a creative artist can be a reasonable citizen in both the republic of letters and the commonwealth. Just as he could advise a federal commission defining an Alaskan wilderness, so he could speak and write for Stanford's first big fund-raising campaign.

In a way that seemed to make his version of western realism useful to a program in creative writing, Stegner's teaching as well as his fiction seemed to eschew the self-indulgence of Thomas Wolfe and the didacticism of James T. Farrell. A novelist's technique did not need to be "experimental" in order to be vigorous. Social understanding and knowledge of history were not irrelevant to the writing of fiction. One could teach craft and discipline, if not talent or genius.

In the years since I knew Stegner as a colleague, I have learned to see more clearly that this kind of balance has an ideological significance. On the one hand I see Stegner and Yvor Winters—despite their sharp differences in principle and personality—as representative challenges to the New York intellectuals whose recent memoirs assume that the only choice for progressive Americans during the Great Depression lay between Stalin and Trotsky. Even in the 1930s these westerners never divided the larger political world into a choice between fascism and some version of Marxism. Just as Stegner could write with critical sympathy about Joe Hill and the International Workers of the World—and still more critically about the forces that destroyed them—so he had deplored the cycles of boom and bust but had believed that the New Deal could minimize suffering and oppression. Of course I have always known that there were many Marxists in California and non-Marxist progressives in New York, but my two western colleagues have come to represent for me the millions who did not need to react in the 1950s and 1960s against the radical allegiance of their youth.

3

By the time I arrived at Stanford, Winters and Stegner had already settled into the virtual truce that enabled them to work in the same program. How they negotiated the truce I don't know, and I can only imagine the battles that preceded it: Winters and some of his students were capable of fierce denunciations when evaluating poets, and disagreement over a fellowship application might have been irresistibly provocative even if a director had not known, as Stegner did, that he himself had absolute control over the Stegner fellowships. One may infer the intensity of the feelings from one of Stegner's responses to an interviewer more than fifteen years after Winters had retired. Not even when asked whether "more novelists or poets" applied for the Wallace Stegner writing fellowships does Stegner mention Winters:

> We had a little bias in favor of fiction, partly because we had more people to teach fiction and partly because I was running the program and was more interested in fiction. We had two poets every year and four fiction writers. In terms of numbers, we had many more applications for fiction while I was still teaching. I think later that

> changed, during the time when Donald Davie was here. Donald, I think, had about as many applications in poetry as Dick Scowcroft had in fiction. But while I was doing it, in any given year we'd have maybe two hundred and fifty applicants, of whom two hundred would be fiction and fifty poetry. Out of those we would pick six. It was a kind of fine strainer.*

Winters, moreover, had recently described Robert Frost as a "spiritual drifter" who had lived up to his great talent in only a few poems, and Frost was offended when Winters declined to attend a reception in Frost's honor at Stegner's house after a reading at Stanford. My thoughts about Winters's irascibility will appear more appropriately in the next chapter. Here I want to observe that, both although and because my two eminent elders disagreed when evaluating poets, Stegner allowed Winters to choose the one or two poetry fellows each year; Stegner and his associate director, Richard Scowcroft, chose the fellows in fiction.

Yet some of us could see beyond Stegner's and Winters's differences a firm area of agreement. Nowhere does that agreement seem more memorable to me than in their responses to two senior appointments in 1961 that brought me distinguished new older colleagues who had been teaching in New England: Irving Howe and Albert J. Guerard.

IRVING HOWE

Howe had been an interdepartmental committee's unanimous choice to occupy the first William Robertson Coe chair in American literature and American studies. Two historians already held Coe chairs. But before Howe could be formally invited, the English department, which had concurred in his nomination to the

*Wallace Stegner and Richard W. Etulain, *Conversations with Wallace Stegner on Western History and Literature* (Salt Lake City: University of Utah Press, 1983), p. 140.

chair, was suddenly asked to withdraw that nomination and instead recommend Howe to be simply professor of English and American literature. Attorneys for the Stanford administration had decided that Howe must be considered ineligible for a Coe chair, because he described himself as coeditor of *Dissent: a Journal of Socialist Opinion*.

Virgil Whitaker, executive head of our department, asked us to treat the requested change as a formality and approve it without debate, but Stegner and Winters agreed heartily with me that the request violated Howe's academic freedom. None of us, not Whitaker himself, had known that the Coe bequest specified the purpose for which the endowment of more than a million dollars was to be used: to establish and maintain a program of American studies "designed to combat in a positive and affirmative way the threat of communism, socialism, totalitarianism, collectivism, and other ideologies opposed to our American System of Free Enterprise."

Whitaker argued that since we were still eager to welcome Howe to the faculty the proposed change would not actually restrict his academic freedom. Probably Whitaker and President Sterling believed that they were merely acknowledging the need to admit both saints and sinners to the community; it seemed to me then, however, that they were following the principle that I have since heard attributed (with variations) to John D. Rockefeller and Booker T. Washington: "The only taint on money is 'tain't enough." Whitaker and Sterling believed we could have both Howe and our share of the Coe money.

Stegner, Winters, and all the specialists in American literature endorsed a letter that I had drafted for the English department to send to President Sterling. With slight revision all the tenured members of the department approved it at our next meeting. We said that we would not teach in a program designed to accomplish political ends, and we insisted somewhat casuistically that the only positive and affirmative way to combat the threats named in the bequest would be to encourage free inquiry and declare that all our decisions on academic appointments would be free of political tests. We reminded the president that Stanford had specifically invited Howe to be considered for a Coe chair. We felt sure that Howe would scorn the demotion to a mere professorship and that Stanford would incur practical damage as well as a loss of principle. Only two years had passed since the eruption of a scandal over Coe-like political language defining the purposes of the Hoover Institution, and over Herbert Hoover's rejection of several distinguished nominees for the vacant directorship.

Our colleagues patiently rejected my truculent suggestion that Stanford return the Coe money if Howe should remain ineligible for the chair. (I did not learn until recently that the University of Minnesota had rejected a similar endowment from the Coe Foundation.) Whitaker, who controlled the budget, pointed his finger at me and asked, "Would you give up a thousand dollars of *your* salary?" But Stegner, Winters, and the other Americanists had all endorsed the original draft. Without the support of those two eminent antagonists, we would probably have failed to achieve even the shrewd compromise that was worked out by Albert Bowker, the canny and humane vice-provost. Since no Coe chair in literature had yet been inaugurated, Bowker promised that the relevant Coe money would be used, without ideological restrictions, to buy books for the library's collection in American studies. Howe would be paid out of funds thus released, and there would be no Coe professor of American literature.

Howe surprised me and delighted us all by agreeing to join us, and from the very beginning of his two years at Stanford he proved to be an extraordinarily valuable colleague. Neither the easterners nor the westerners among us were intellectually inactive. We could see too the strong personal nature of the energy that radiated from Howe's presence in the room. Yet we all welcomed that energy as a regional importation. It came from the East—not just from Waltham, Massachusetts, but from New York.

If there was any condescension in Howe's attitude toward our provincial campus, it was of a kind that would have irritated

Stegner much less than the precious snobbery associated with Stegner's notion of the "literary" set. Howe spoke and wrote about the politics of the real world as well as *The Politics of the Novel* (at that time the most influential of his books). He was open and direct. I remember clearly two of his blunt declarations of astonishment: he found it hard to believe that the Stanford library did not subscribe to *Dissent,* and with a disarming smile, making himself the target of his joke, he said he was amazed to learn that some of the half-naked, suntanned young men who played catch with a football on the front lawns of their fraternity houses could also write intelligent analyses of difficult poems. "They're so big," he protested. "How could they be so bright?"

A fair part of Howe's impact on Stanford must be attributed to the range of his interests. He had already published books on Faulkner, Sherwood Anderson, and the CIO, and essays on a number of major European writers. He broadened the range of discourse with allusions to nineteenth- and twentieth-century European political thought. He began teaching courses on American poets, Dickinson, Frost, and Stevens. On Winters's recommendation he developed an interest in Frederick Goddard Tuckerman. And of course Howe continued to review contemporary fiction. Yet the main quality brought to the Stanford Farm by this fast-talking New Yorker, who in a one-hour lecture could read ten or fifteen more pages than any of us, was political.

I don't mean that he was trying to convert students or colleagues to his version of socialism. The best word I can find for the central quality is engagement. The best images in which my memory depicts the drastic changes at Stanford during the 1960s show Howe in action. Look at him first in the spring of 1963, when Stanford has only recently abolished the rule forbidding visiting speakers to address "controversial" topics unless qualified opponents are present on stage to debate the issues. During Martin Luther King's campaign against segregation in Birmingham, the novelist James Baldwin has spoken at Stanford on civil rights, concluding with an appeal for funds. As hundreds crowd forward to contribute, student marshals move in to enforce a rule against political fund-raising on campus. But before they can push through to confront the undergraduate who has been breaking the rule, Irving Howe's long arm reaches over two or three heads and Howe grabs the basket of money. "I'll take the responsibility," he says, and the marshals withdraw as bills and coins continue to flow into the basket.

As late as 1963, such a gesture was still noteworthy. A committed professor, recently arrived from the East, could set a mild example of civil disobedience, or at least raise the question whether rules set by the dean of students bound the faculty as well. By the time Howe returned as a visiting speaker a few years later, he no longer represented new engagement. He stood for the Old Left, and many unruly partisans of the New filled the lecture hall with their new styles of dress and vociferous response. Howe had not changed. Standing behind the lectern in Dinkelspiel Hall, he remains, in my memory, just as firmly committed to civil rights as he was when he seized the basket after James Baldwin's lecture, and now he deplores American policy in southeast Asia. But whereas the most impassioned challenge to Baldwin's lecture comes from the student who asks, "But Mr. Baldwin, where can we find any hope?" (to which Baldwin answers promptly, "You must be a *very* young man"), Howe's loudest critics show that they scorn his commitment to civility and to rational debate, which many of them regard as instruments of the oppressor. Howe admonishes them with a witty equivalent of the argument he has used against revolutionaries at Hunter College: "In six years you'll be a den-tist." His wit has won a point, but he looks sad.

My first glimpse of that expression, on the night Howe arrived in California, made me fear that (as Stegner had predicted) he wouldn't stay with us very long. I could see when I met him under the ghastly fluorescent lights at the San Francisco airport that his arrival as an immigrant to California was much gloomier than mine had been. And his entry into South Palo Alto was even worse than S. Levin's arrival in Oregon, in Malamud's *A New Life*.

At nine o'clock on that hot Sunday evening, everything in the California Avenue business district was dark. Except for a bank on the corner of El Camino Real, one could not see a building more than two stories high. At the hotel in which a frugal friend had advised Howe to reserve a room, we carried the baggage up a narrow stairway and noticed that some men seated along the wall on the ground floor were watching a television set that was mounted under the stairs. The night-time manager met us at the registration desk upstairs and showed us to a windowless room so small that the three of us and the luggage could not have stood if I had not left the door open. I cannot forget the wretched, surprised look on Howe's face as he learned that no larger room existed and then that no, he could not now find within walking distance a place to get a cup of coffee. He declined my invitation to stay at my house for a few days, but he did agree to let Pat help him find an apartment the next day. Although he did learn to enjoy the pleasures of the Bay Area, his first night in the new land must have given him an unforgettable impression of the distance between Manhattan and South Palo Alto.

Stegner did not say "I told you so" when Howe announced that he would be leaving us for the City University of New York, but he did have Texan origins and midwestern experience in mind, along with other qualities, when he nominated his old friend Claude Simpson as Howe's successor. I acknowledged Simpson's solid reputation but said we should seek someone who had written more books; Stegner suggested dryly that we might call Simpson the Coe Wheelhorse of American Literature. When I reminded Stegner recently that I had been wrong—Simpson turned out to be an invaluable and beloved colleague—the reply was gracious: "I knew him, and you didn't."

Yes, we did accept the establishment of a Coe chair after all. Bowker was gone (to be chancellor of CUNY) and Humanities and Sciences also had a new dean, Robert Sears, to whom our scruples now seemed like theological hairsplitting. Sears denied that the offensive clause in the Coe bequest would be used invidiously in the future; the question of a nominee's political views would simply not come up. Simpson graciously told us that although he had no objection to accepting the chair with Sears's assurances of complete liberty, he could understand our feelings about the issue and would abide by our judgment. With varying degrees of reluctance, then, we all acquiesced. Uncomfortable as we all felt about the withdrawal of Howe's nomination and the reintroduction of the Coe name, I am certain that neither of Howe's successors has had to endure so much as a hint of political interference. I try to believe that even if a future nominee for the chair should bear a name tied prominently to the word *socialism,* Stanford's attorneys and administrators will let the winds of freedom blow.

ALBERT J. GUERARD

In a different way from Irving Howe's nomination, Albert Guerard's arrival in 1961 highlighted some surprising points of agreement between Stegner and Winters. Neither when selecting fellows nor when inviting guests to lecture or to replace him for a term did Stegner often choose writers who could be called experimental, postmodern, unconventional. I do remember that John Barth, Philip Roth, and Saul Bellow came to speak or read from their work, but the prevailing voices I hear echoing from those decades express the resonant reasonableness of Frank O'Connor, Robert Frost, and Walter Van Tilburg Clark. Most memorable for me among the visiting writers who actually taught courses were Clark, Malcolm Cowley (who spent two different years at Stanford), Janet Lewis, and the Welsh novelist Richard Jones, who became my good friend when we met again at the University of Virginia. Perhaps Kenneth Rexroth, who visited for a summer term, and Hortense Calisher were the most nearly unorthodox writers among the visiting professors.

Any graduate program in writing will attract some students who either resist instruction or test the limits set by the authorities. During the 1950s and 1960s, as beatniks, hippies, and then the New Left flourished, Stanford received its full share. But if Ken Kesey and Gwen Davis had the greatest commercial success and the revolutionary members of Venceremos stirred the circulation most powerfully, the good writers whose work Stegner prized as the program's characteristic achievements were Evan Connell, Wendell Berry, Robin White, and Eugene Burdick.

These preferences caused no major controversies that I was aware of until Albert J. Guerard joined the faculty in 1961. At Harvard Guerard had encouraged young novelists of manners—Alison Lurie was writing stories in his course when I took it in 1946—and his own novels clearly identified him as a realist. But he took greatest pride and pleasure from nurturing rebels, experimenters, antirealists. He delighted in talking about Camus and Robbe-Grillet, and the former student whose fiction he admired most was John Hawkes.

The situation at Stanford was complicated on both sides by the knowledge that in leaving Harvard Guerard was coming home. He had grown up on the campus as the son and namesake of a distinguished professor. Yvor Winters had accepted Guerard's first short story for publication in *Hound and Horn* when Guerard was only sixteen, and Winters had directed Guerard's doctoral dissertation in English literature. Now, as Guerard returned to the western provinces from his professorship at Harvard, hints or suspicions of condescension glanced off the sandstone walls of the Inner Quad. Guerard protested hyperbolically that nothing in the Stanford English department had changed in the two decades since his departure. He insisted on bringing the modern more emphatically into the curriculum. He mounted a campaign to abolish the requirement that all doctoral students learn to read Old and Middle English. When that campaign failed, he succeeded in establishing an alternative program in comparative literature, administered within the English department but substituting mastery of another modern language (and much of its literature) for the old philological requirements. Soon afterward he gained approval for a doctoral program in modern thought and literature, which has flourished now for nearly a quarter of a century. He wanted to devise a graduate program that would nurture at least as many men of letters (modeled on Edmund Wilson) as factual scholars (modeled at their limited best, in Guerard's conception, on George Lyman Kittredge).

With equally vigorous ingenuity, Guerard challenged convictions about writing. Neither Stegner nor Winters, whose prescriptive principles Guerard had renounced, welcomed his eagerness to encourage the avant garde. Guerard volunteered to serve as director of freshman English. Soon he established some sections of creative writing in the third quarter of the required composition course. Then he was either forbidden or simply not invited to teach the advanced courses in fiction writing that he had often taught at Harvard. He pressed on. In collaboration with John Hawkes of Brown University, Guerard's conviction that every freshman writer should develop a personal voice produced not only an anthology (*The Personal Voice*) but a federally subsidized curricular experiment, the Voice Project.

Aside from technical innovations designed to help each student discover an authentic expository voice, the chief institutional effect of the Voice Project was the mobilization of a squad of writers from the East Coast. At first the project could support a year's visit from Hawkes as director, and other well-established writers —the dramatist and poet William Alfred from Harvard, the short-story writer Sylvia Berkman from Wellesley, the novelist Mitchell Goodman from New York—taught in the program for a brief time. The arrival of these writers intensified the sense of excitement that new political issues, the civil rights movement and the Vietnam war, had already stimulated in the English department. Typical of the project's innovations was the Freshman Film Series, a weekly screening directed by Clive Miller, who produced stacks of mimeographed commentary for each occasion and presided, sometimes hilariously, by firing a barrage of trivia over the heads of an adoring audience. For a time the innovations made one or two hundred students feel that they were united in a pioneering enterprise.

To Stegner the project and the subsequent appointment of several younger writers must have seemed like an invasion. Guerard called these novelists writer-teachers. Remembering Harvard's Briggs-Copeland fund for hiring a young poet or novelist, he justified their appointment as one way of infusing vitality and variety into a freshman year that too often reduces initial eagerness to sophomoric boredom. Very young writers who had actually published a novel or a book of stories might invigorate the required course that was usually taught by assistant professors and graduate students committed to scholarship. But of course the arrival of Jay Neugeborn, Jerome Charyn, Clive Miller, James Beuchler (three at a time, on annual appointments which could be renewed twice) meant that writers chosen by the criteria of Albert Guerard had access to prospective majors in creative writing before the students were eligible to take courses in the program directed by Wallace Stegner.

My own reaction to these innovations continues to puzzle me. Although I did not believe that the Voice Project would succeed either in establishing a new principle of instruction or in preventing the sophomore slump, I welcomed all the new writers. Skeptical though I was about Voice, I could not deny that many students involved in the program loved the experience. The difference between the novelists' emphasis and that of our doctoral candidates and assistant professors would surely add variety to the composition course and to the department's intellectual life. Surely, too, the newly energetic attention centered on the required freshman course, the directorship of which had often been foisted on a junior member of the faculty, would improve the morale of many instructors and students. Much as I admired Stegner, Winters, and Scowcroft, moreover, my approval of their respective ways of teaching creative writing could not overcome my conviction that it ought to be good for the university to have a variety of models for students and a variety of paths for the students' development into creative artists. I did not know how to institutionalize the unconventional, the experimental, or the revolutionary, or how to standardize originality, but I believed then as I do now that an intellectual community would be strengthened if it could welcome talented innovators—even when they challenge some of its own established ideas.

Where then is the puzzle? I simply see that my conviction was too abstract. It took too little account of complexities both psychological and institutional. Since I still enjoy the luxury of not having to decide how a creative writing program will be administered, I can wish that Guerard had been welcomed to teach creative writing at Stanford, and I can be glad that our community had the benefit of his squad of novelists. Yet my fondness and respect for Guerard cannot erase a memory of his restless, unrelenting efforts to change departmental policy in those years. Had he been brought into the creative writing program, his efforts to change it would almost surely have gone beyond his being assigned to teach in it. At what point was Stegner to exert his authority to defend his convictions? I am left, not for the first time, with conflicting judgments.

Winters's concurrence with Stegner on Guerard's curricular initiatives can be described much more briefly. Winters told me he was proud of his former student's achievement, but of course he deplored Guerard's encouragement of what Winters considered romantic self-indulgence and obscurantism. Probably he also felt, though he did not express to me, a measure of personal rejection in Guerard's apostasy from Wintersian reason to psychoanalytical insight. Winters himself had fought for inclusion of the modern and of modern European languages in the literary curriculum, but he saw Guerard's proposed and enacted innovations as part of a complex threat to disciplined learning.

In supporting Howe and resisting Guerard, then, both Winters and Stegner showed that their sometimes vehement differences did not preclude fundamental agreement about civil liberties and the curriculum. Stegner must have gritted his teeth when he delegated to Winters the annual nomination of two poetry fellows. He thought that Winters's principles of selection were far too rigid, and that the condescension of some Wintersian students was insufferable. ("Kittredge was tolerable," he told me once, when one of Winters's students had offended him; "what people couldn't stand was all those little Kattridges.") Yet he and Winters stood firmly—some thought rigidly—against what they both considered assaults upon standards.

4

Imagining the strong personal feelings that must have been aroused by his decisions concerning Winters and Guerard reminds me that although much of what I learned from Stegner was decidedly professional, the most important lessons highlighted the personal in the professional. Of course I am grateful for his generous hospitality and for nominating me for fellowships and valuable editorial assignments. But both as an admonition and as a worthy example he taught me unintentionally when he was provoked to express his vulnerability.

Stegner attached to the "last of the western sticks" some of the most precious values that I thought I had inhaled with the Colonial and Revolutionary air of York, P-A. He made his most succinct declaration of this credo in "Born a Square: The Westerner's Dilemma," which laments the plight of young western writers in the 1960s and implicitly advises them to write about what they know from their own earliest experience, even if that unfashionably innocent, hopeful, and middle-class experience will not bring great critical or financial reward. I believe I first heard this essay as a lecture called "Us Christians Ain't Got No Lions"; I am certain that I heard Stegner tell the story of a weeping Roman boy who refused to be consoled by his parents' assurance that the gladiators were bound to die whether or not they chose to fight. "But Mother," the boy cries as he points, "that Christian ain't got no lion." The Protestant westerner's dilemma, Stegner argues in

"Born a Square," is that if he writes what is true to his experience he will not find readers, and if he tries to imitate James Baldwin, Norman Mailer, Tennessee Williams, or Saul Bellow, he will fail from inauthenticity.

The tone of "Born a Square" varies from satirical hyperbole to rueful lament to guarded hopefulness. Surely some of Stegner's impatience with young writers whom he calls "the literary, who are schooled in the torments, emptiness, and weary kicks of life," was provoked by naïve students' efforts to imitate "expatriates, beats, faggots, junkies, Southerners committed to Gothic guilts and erratic violences, Negroes remembering three hundred years of labeled or *de facto* slavery, Jews remembering a thousand years of ghettoes and pogroms." How could the young western writer produce what seemed to be required in the 1960s? "Imagine as he may how he might feel if he were a Jew, [for example,] he knows he is no Jew, doesn't think like one and can't feel like one, has neither the cultural stamina nor the special humor nor the special masochism" (p. 47).

But of course *Wolf Willow,* published less than two years before "Born a Square," made it perfectly clear that Stegner's complaint referred as well to his own historical predicament. *Wolf Willow* makes one of the most moving statements I have ever seen of an American westerner's feeling of alienation from the European history that dominates his cultural education. As a middle-aged writer discovering the local past of the Cypress Hills in Saskatchewan, Stegner felt irritated by "the very richness of that past." He resented having "been cheated of it"—of "Fort Walsh, and all that story of buffalo hunter, Indian and half-breed, Mounted Policeman and wolfer, which came to its climax just here"—when he had really needed it in his childhood. For a past to which he could be "tribally and emotionally committed," he had felt forced to choose between the Civil War, in which his paternal grandfather had fought, and the Norway from which his maternal grandparents had emigrated: "Being a mama's boy, I chose Norway, which made a real hash of my affiliations. All through my childhood I signed my most private books and documents with the Norwegian name that my grandfather had given up on coming to America. It seems to me now an absurdity that I should have felt it necessary to go as far as the Hardanger Fjord for a sense of belonging" (pp. 111–12).

What moves me in these pages even as I reread them now is more than Stegner's fine evocation of "the Plains people, a people of many tribes but one culture," all those tribes whose rich way of life ended there. For me, the native of York, P-A, who had embraced the local past at least partly because it had powerful meaning in my early education, Stegner's most poignant line declared that all of his region's past "was legitimately mine, I walked that earth, but none of [this past] was known to me." The past of the Nez Perce, the Blackfoot, and the others did legitimately belong to Stegner. I cheered his forthright claim to it, just as I applauded James Baldwin's acknowledgment in *Notes of a Native Son* that Afro-American identity is extremely complex, and Baldwin's sober discovery that he himself was a native son.

But in the very days during which Stegner was writing "Born a Square," I had been writing an appreciative essay that nonetheless questioned one major trope: Baldwin's insistence that Shakespeare, Dante, and the cathedral at Chartres can be understood by illiterate Swiss villagers in a way that a black man can never equal. I rejected Baldwin's declaration that if we go back five hundred years we find those illiterate villagers "in their glory, but I am on the shores of Africa, waiting for the conquerors to arrive."* I sympathized with both Stegner's and Baldwin's feeling that American education had imposed an alien past upon them, different though they were in genealogy and temperament. And of course I sympathized with Stegner's predicament as an excellent writer who was respected but often overlooked as a regional realist, whose books

*See "Baldwin's Autobiographical Essays: The Problem of Negro Identity," *Massachusetts Review* 5 (Winter 1964): 239–47.

sometimes won national prizes but were critically undervalued by the *New York Times Book Review*.

Yet when I confronted Baldwin's preliterate "I" on the shores of Africa, I found it conceptually incomplete. The literate part of his identity could not be excised. His mastery of the English language and his awareness of history made him related to Shakespeare and Dante in a way that the illiterate Swiss villagers could not approach. In making that argument I unwittingly invoked Stegner's hash of affiliations by asking where my own children would go if they were obliged to play his atavistic game—to England, Germany, or Denmark with some of their mother's ancestors, or to the ghettoes and shtetls of eastern Europe with mine?

Stegner's fictive young western persona made me uneasy. I believed that his identical twin could have been found, perhaps even in 1964 and surely in 1940, in hundreds of small towns and cities in Pennsylvania, New York, the Middle West, the South. While I respected the impulse to generalize and classify, long experience inside Jewish life had made me unable to believe that there is such a thing as "think[ing] like one" or "feel[ing] like one." Of course I could see that Stegner referred to a certain ideal type, what the naïve young writer would think of as the typical thoughts and feelings of a Jewish character. In some Jewish writers I could see what Stegner meant by the special humor and the special masochism; in others, however, from George S. Kaufman and S. J. Perelman to the Herman Wouk of *The Caine Mutiny*, the Bernard Malamud of *The Natural*, the Scholem Asch of *The Nazarene*, I could see neither the one nor the other. Thus I found myself sympathizing with Ralph Ellison's protest against a contemporaneous argument of Irving Howe's. Ellison refused to concede that his freedom to write as a literary artist, with a purpose and a technique beyond angry Afro-American protest, depended on Richard Wright's having already expressed Afro-American anger. Ellison claimed the right to express or repress his own anger and (like the Stegner who claimed the Plains Indians) to choose as predecessors not only Afro-American writers but Herman Melville and T. S. Eliot, from whom he had chosen the epigraphs to his own masterpiece.*

From "Born a Square" and *Wolf Willow,* then, I learned that a western Protestant's connection to the local, ethnic, and national past could be just as complex as my own. A man whose birthright seemed to place him comfortably among the vast majority could feel not only that his childhood had been cheated of its true past, but also that his literary voice could be drowned out by shrill cries that make his own more carefully reasoned and balanced work seem too calm and insufficiently alienated. I began to see an affinity among several disparate passages: the closing line of Malamud's *The Assistant* ("All men are Jews"), Baldwin's claim that "the Negro" is the truly representative American, Ellison's memoir of his boyhood in Oklahoma, and Stegner's pleas for his young westerner, for Wright Morris, for himself. I knew even then that I was observing these connections in light of my own allegiance to a complex past. And I remain as grateful for the insight into those connections as for the unfailing personal generosity with which both Wallace and Mary Stegner treated me and my family.

*See Irving Howe, "Black Boys and Native Sons," *Dissent* 10, no. 4 (Autumn 1963): 353–68; and Ralph Ellison, *Shadow and Act* (New York: Random House, 1964), pp. 107–43.

Yvor Winters

When I first met Yvor Winters in 1952, he was nearly fifty-two years old and I was twenty-seven. I could not then have imagined that I would ever dare to write a little memoir about him. Although I hardly knew him, I quickly learned that he felt strongly opposed to narratives about the personal qualities of writers and that he intended to ask his correspondents not to preserve his letters. Ten years after his death, however, I decided it would not be a betrayal of friendship to record some little-known evidence of his value as a friend and colleague.

In those first weeks I would not have dreamed that I could ever *want* to write sympathetically about Winters. The image of him that I had brought with me from Harvard seemed to have been accurate spiritually even though totally wrong visually. From the few of his essays that I had read, and from his reputation as a western curmudgeon, I had expected to meet an ascetic man whose person carried as little fat as his prose. I had not yet read his splendid poem in celebration of California wines. I was surprised to find him a rotund figure with a florid complexion. One could tell even before hearing him speak lovingly about ways to cook chili or prepare escalloped potatoes that this man enjoyed good food. But his conversation was even more serious and spare than I had expected it to be, and in my anxiety as a new colleague on my first full-time appointment I felt threatened by it. I remember very clearly that soon after his first cordial greeting at a reception for new faculty members he suddenly asked me a question about the four American historians on whose work I was writing my Ph.D. thesis: "Which one was the best?"

He did not put the question rudely. I remembered too, that he had treated me generously in unsolicited and very helpful correspondence about living arrangements for my family soon after he had heard about my appointment. But he had so strong a reputation for insisting on firm judgments, and he had put his question so directly, that I fumbled in an embarrassed search for an answer. I had been preoccupied with interpreting the material and with proving relationships among my four historians. I had thought very little about ranking them. They were all interesting, all valuable; what did I care about comparative judgments? I finally brought out my answer, the standard opinion: "I suppose Parkman was the best historian."

"Parkman's the worst," Winters replied, biting down on his pipe; "Motley's the best." His eyes told me that he took some comic pleasure in expressing that unconventional judgment, but I knew, too, that he meant it.

Years later I saw in this first literary conversation an epitome of the most exemplary service that Winters's criticism and his personal conduct performed for me and many others. He not only provoked me to think seriously about value but repeatedly showed me the value in writers I had neglected or underestimated. I often learned, too, from his celebrated or notorious strictures on Whitman, Emerson, Frost, Eliot, and Wallace Stevens, but for me he became much more valuable as a literary rescuer than as an executioner. John Lothrop Motley was only the first of a number of major and minor writers whose worth Winters helped me to appreciate. Although his criticism of Francis Parkman helped me to see some defects that I might otherwise have missed, I did not need to reject Parkman, Frost, or Emerson—nor did Winters himself totally reject any of these writers—in order to perceive the value that Winters showed me in neglected works by Ben Jonson, Jones Very, James Fenimore Cooper, Frederick Goddard Tuckerman, or E. A. Robinson. The scandal of Winters's reputation fed on his vehement denunciations and his idiosyncratic praise. More important to me than whether Tuckerman's "The Cricket" was the best poem of the nineteenth century, or Jones Very a better poet than Emerson, or J. V. Cunningham the best poet now writing in English, is the certain fact that I never knew some excellent works of those writers and others—works as distant from one another as Ben Jonson's "To Heaven" and Janet Lewis's *The Wife of Martin Guerre* and *The Invasion*—until Winters introduced me to them. In the fifteen years of our association, I never heard him praise a literary work in which I failed to find genuine excellence.

That first laconic exchange also left me with the feeling that I was somehow obliged to fill a great barrel of silence, which Winters himself had opened. Even after I had come to know him well, he remained one of several friends who left silences for others to fill, friends whose mute, expectant bearing suggested that their own silence had been provoked by the inadequacy of their interlocutors. Winters was not at ease in idle conversation. He frequently spoke with startling wit, and he was an excellent raconteur, but casual speech often seemed to make him uncomfortable. He preferred to write, and he often did. Two instances that occurred during my first months at Stanford will illustrate the range of this preference.

At lunch one day with several other colleagues, I happened to fill one of those silences with some chatter about our pregnant cocker spaniel. Winters, whose office wall displayed a photograph of himself with one of his champion Airedales, remarked jovially that a cocker spaniel is not a dog, and then, in what I took to be the same tone, he asked me whether I knew how to construct a whelping box. The conversation ended in general laughter when I said I had never heard of such a thing. The next morning I found in my mailbox at the Department of English a three-page, single-spaced letter from Winters, with lucid instructions for making a whelping box, attaching the burlap, getting the dog accustomed to the box, and helping with the birth in an emergency. Without that explicit letter, we would surely have lost one of the puppies that were born in our whelping box two weeks later, for an emergency did occur and the instructions helped us to revive an apparently stillborn puppy.

The other episode was somewhat less pleasant at the time, and I still have mixed feelings about it, although I did belatedly learn that my presence in Winters's seminar must have made him uncomfortable. Winters offered one of the few courses anywhere on the literature of historiography, a two-term graduate seminar called American Historians as Men of Letters. I had asked him to let me audit his informal lectures during the first term, for I had completed my research and was now writing my Harvard thesis *in absentia,* on several of the historians considered in his seminar. The class was held in his office, a large, dark room on the ground floor of Building 40 in the Inner Quad. The memorable features of the room, besides the Airedale prize photograph and one or two other pictures on the wall, were the very high ceiling and the old Morris chair in which Winters could often be seen reading as one passed the open doorway; there must also have been a desk and some kind of seminar table, but these have been supplanted in my memory by the much more elegant furniture that was crowded in, along with the Morris chair, when the office was shrunk and the ceiling lowered seven or eight years later. Winters sat behind his desk and lectured from notes jotted inside the front cover of a book by William H. Prescott. His notes must have consisted largely of page numbers; looking up at the four or five students, he would make a few precise and coherent remarks, including both biographical information and critical judgments, and then he would open the book to a marked page, read a few lines of Prescott to us, and comment further. When he had finished, he asked me whether I had any comment to make on his judgments. I had nothing to say then, but in a brief private discussion after class I told him I had evidence to show that Motley, whom Winters had praised in contrast to Prescott, had been guilty of some of the same evasions, anti-Catholic prejudices, and critical fallacies for which Winters had justly but severely criticized Prescott. Before we parted, Winters expressed some interest in seeing my evidence.

He opened the next meeting of the seminar by reading a long typewritten statement that he had written since the time of our last conversation. In the extensive preamble he explained that he had for years been teaching courses ranging over the whole history of English poetry and of literary criticism; he had dared to teach this course in historiography only because the worthy subject had been neglected. Mr. Levin, he said, "professionally trained in a large eastern university," had had time to specialize in American subjects and in history as well as literature. But of course the overworked, self-taught, western amateur had an answer for the professionally trained easterner, and that argument in itself was very strong. The issue had to do with absolute and relative standards of historical judgment, and Motley, forthright in recognizing and expressing the severity of his judgments against tyrants and bigots, had the better of Prescott, whose allegedly flexible standards of judgment tended both to weaken any basis for moral judgment and to disguise his own ethnocentric prejudices.

I was distressed to find myself in this predicament. Only a few weeks after dragging my family all the way from Boston, the Hub of the Universe, to the toe of Mrs. Weston's continent, I had provoked my notoriously opinionated senior colleague to write an extraordinary paper that seemed to set me on high for the pleasure of seeing me tumble down. And of course I felt the more uncomfortable for knowing, as the students in the seminar surely knew, that my professional training would not be complete until I submitted an acceptable thesis to the large eastern university.

When I decided not to beard Winters in front of his students, but to write up my evidence and give the paper to him after the term had ended, I misjudged him. A few days later he reminded me of my statement that I had some evidence to contradict his comparative judgments of the historians, and he insisted that I read it to the seminar. Since the question was largely factual, my demonstration that Motley, too, had sometimes conveniently used a shifting standard of judgment brought another long silence to that dark room. Eventually Winters said, "Thank you," and those were the last words I ever heard from him on the subject. Only from a colleague did I learn, more than a year afterward, that Winters had expressed pleasure at my willingness to disagree with him.

2

That "Thank you" and the other laconic comments I have remembered here were only a few of the observations by which the combination of Winters's characteristic brevity and his willingness to judge established his role among his colleagues. Although I became his friend and worked closely with him for more than twelve years, and although he read and approved of my scholarly and critical work, he did not talk to me about the things that mattered most to him. These were questions of poetry and philosophy, and it was to these that he referred when he told me, on more than one occasion, but with no intent to wound me even though we both knew his remark was excluding me from a select company, that there were only two colleagues on our faculty with whom he could really talk.

The most emphatic demonstration of Winters's laconic judgment of his colleagues occurred in a private conversation that another friend reported to me. Winters had been provoked by some departmental controversy to observe (in an epithet from the 1920s) that an absent colleague was full of banana oil. My informant, who felt unwilling to consent by silence to so strong a condemnation of the colleague, struggled to think of a virtue that Winters might also recognize in the man, and he heard himself protesting weakly that the colleague in question was at least sincere. Winters's reply, I was told, was instantaneous: "He's sincerely full of banana oil."

Long before my arrival at Stanford, the relationship of Winters to the other senior members of the English department had been established through reciprocal judgments that, though less emphatic than the comment on banana oil, were nonetheless mutually condescending. Of course there were individual exceptions in both friendship and hostility, but in general Winters and his senior colleagues had tacitly conceded spheres of academic influence across borders defined by mutual respect and condescension. Winters had a deep respect for literary scholarship and for the learning of some of his colleagues. Throughout the time of our association he consistently opposed efforts to abolish or reduce various scholarly courses that had traditionally been required for the Ph.D. in English, and he regularly advised young poets to take courses in the history of their language, in other languages, and in the history of English and American literature. Yet he believed and he had said publicly that many of his colleagues had no informed interest in contemporary poetry or in major philosophical issues, and that most of them were indifferent to the implications of their philosophical beliefs. He sent his students to learn what could be learned from those colleagues, but everyone knew that the best of his students had access to a world the professors could not enter.

By 1952, all his colleagues knew that Winters had won international distinction with both his criticism and his poems. His prize from the National Institute of Arts and Letters was only the latest accolade. These colleagues were not the men who had held back Winters's promotion to a full professorship until he was fifty years old. They admired his intelligence, at least some of his poems, and the strength of his prose, and they seemed genuinely fond of him. Yet they condescended to what they considered his eccentric judgments, they understandably resented his blunt public statements about their own collective inadequacies, and they were sometimes outraged by the presumption of a Winters student. They conceded to Winters virtually total control of advanced instruction in twentieth-century poetry and American literature. The only senior professors who taught American literature during my first few years at Stanford were Winters and Stegner, both of whom, though they had earned Ph.D. degrees, were primarily known as creative writers. The subjects that were conceded to Winters were subjects about which his traditionalist colleagues cared relatively little. Until about 1960, moreover, it was easy for a Stanford graduate student to earn a Ph.D. in English without having read a single work of American literature, or even of English literature after the 1870s, the decade in which the nineteenth century was decreed to have ended.

The ceremony at which a newcomer had a chance to observe these relationships, which were much more complex than my crude generalizations can indicate, was a luncheon meeting known as the Klatsch. Every day at noon Winters would stroll across the hall from his office to the even larger and darker room shared by the two senior philologists, Herbert D. Meritt and Robert W. Ackerman. Hung with tapestries and crowded with books, including the department's copy of the multivolume Oxford New English Dictionary, this office was shaded by the colonnades that protect Stanford's central quadrangle from brilliant sun through most of the year and from steady rains in the winter. My memory probably exaggerates the darkness of the room at noon on sunny days, and I surely err in remembering the still atmosphere as if it had come from Hawthorne's Custom House, or Varner's store in *The Hamlet,* or Nicholas Vedder's inn in "Rip Van Winkle." Many lively and delightful conversations and some very serious ones occurred during the hundreds of noon hours that several of us passed there in the company of Winters, our genial hosts the philologists, and two or three other professors. But I am sure my recollection of Winters's presence in those meetings is accurate. He always sat in the straight oak chair that filled the space between the doorway and the heavy volumes of the New English Dictionary, and one or two of those volumes were usually open on the tilted reading shelf just to the right of his ruddy face. He never ate lunch but quietly smoked his pipe as we ate our sandwiches. A vigorous gardener in those days, and the proud cultivator of at least one specimen of every fruit tree native to northern California, he was nonetheless a portly figure, and he seemed almost to sag into the chair as he puffed gravely or smiled over his pipe.

He was also the central figure. Sometimes he joined in the banter and the anecdotal conversation, but his characteristic role, which he and his fellow professors established collaboratively, was that of an eccentric adversary whom they provoked to answer piquant questions about his bizarre opinions, or who challenged them with new judgments or with new questions about the opinions they already knew. He would often begin his part of these colloquies by addressing us all as "my learned colleagues" or "you professors." Most of these exchanges were friendly and even jovial; these men shared with Winters memories of academic life in the 1930s, when they had all occupied desks in a great room called the bull pen, when their salaries had been fixed at $1,600 a year, and when the standard teaching load had been five sections of freshman English, with 125–150 themes to be read each week. (Exhausted by my unsuccessful efforts to write my thesis under a teaching load of three sections and 75–80 themes a week, I once asked Winters when he had found time to write his critical essays during the 1930s, and he promptly answered, "Two o'clock in the morning.") Sometimes, however, the air would seem to vibrate, as it did when Winters, having challenged the value of Gray's "Elegy" or Thomson's "The Seasons," refused to accept a colleague's appeal to "the standard judgment" but insisted on hearing the man's own judgment and the reasons for it.

Exciting, too, in a different way, was Winters's unforgettable account of the Lamson case, the conviction, later overturned by the California Supreme Court, of a Stanford University Press editor for the alleged murder of his wife. Winters's account of the circumstantial evidence on which a county prosecutor convicted Lamson led to a splendid exposition of the circumstantial evidence that proved Lamson could not have killed his wife in the manner required by the prosecutor's case. I was one of the two or three new colleagues for whom Winters was persuaded by the veterans of the Klatsch to tell that story once again; and when he came to the grisly behavior of some Stanford administrators and a Stanford Medical School pathologist in the prosecution of an innocent man, we newcomers had to notice both Winters's total absorption in the narrative, and his veteran auditors' mixture of admiration and amused detachment. Here, they seemed to feel, is our distinguished zealot, who can still work up a passion over issues that would not have impassioned us even when they were current nearly twenty years ago. The tension of Winters's narrative was destroyed by one of these veterans just as Winters was describing the Lamsons' bathroom so that we could understand the circumstantial evidence to prove Mrs. Lamson had not been beaten to death but had fallen in the tub. "Now here is the bathtub," Winters said, gesturing toward one desk, "and here is the door."

"Then what's that that Herb's sitting on?" asked an irreverent colleague who had heard the story before. Winters lost no dignity or emphasis when he continued his narrative after the laughter had subsided.

I stopped attending the Klatsch in 1959, when I moved to the Stanford campus, quit smoking, gained weight, and decided to try lunching more abstemiously at home. As I rode my bicycle into the Inner Quad at 12:45 one afternoon, I saw a fire engine and an ambulance backed up to the door of Building 40. As I was dismounting, four firemen labored to get a heavy stretcher-load through the door and into the ambulance. They had loosened Winters's tie and collar. Winters smiled up at me and asked whether I wanted to go for a ride. In the ambulance he told me that he had fainted during the Klatsch—"from simple boredom," he declared. "What other escape does one have?" In the emergency room at the Stanford Hospital, Winters insisted on giving the doctor the same explanation; he said he had used the same desperate measure more than once when the boredom had become intolerable.

3

Since I heard Winters tell the Lamson story in the autumn of 1952, when we were also discussing the first Eisenhower-Stevenson campaign, I never doubted that in politics he was a liberal who had supported the New Deal and the Fair Deal. Not until I had known him for several years did I learn that an article in *American Scholar* had referred to him as a Fascist (whereupon Winters had resigned from Phi Beta Kappa), and that Leslie Fiedler had convicted him (by association) of being a conservative Catholic gentleman! Many people simply assumed that this "absolutist" and "reactionary" critic must be a political reactionary. But Winters had belonged to the American Civil Liberties Union of Northern California ever since its founding in the mid-1930s. He was a life member of the National Association for the Advancement of Colored People. He had spoken and acted in defense of Japanese-American citizens who were sent to detention camps during World War II. In the autumn of 1952 he endorsed a letter that many Columbia University faculty members had published in criticism of General Eisenhower's presidency of Columbia. When more than a hundred Stanford faculty members gave money and signed their names to publish a copy of that letter in the local newspaper, a great roar of indignation in the press and the university deplored the enormity of our having associated the name of Stanford with a political campaign. In those days no political speeches were allowed on the Stanford campus, none more political than Herbert Hoover's allegedly nonpartisan addresses. When Hoover's private secretary, who had concentrated in English as an undergraduate long ago, threatened publicly to monitor the future conduct of the new young English instructors who had signed the infamous letter, Winters went out of his way to reassure us.

In the fourteen years between my arrival and his retirement, Winters proved the validity of these credentials in several incidents that in one way or another brought together his literary or professional judgment and his humane attitude toward social issues. At a meeting of the Stanford chapter of the American Association of University Professors during the worst days of McCarthyism, for example, Winters spoke forcibly in defense of a Communist's right to teach—so long as particular doctrines did not vitiate one's ability to teach one's subject, as Winters believed certain forms of Marxist literary criticism would do. He insisted then (as he did several years later in our defense of Irving Howe's eligibility for a Coe chair) that candidates for new appointments be judged according to their professional work, and of course that tenure rights be respected.

Later on in the 1950s, Winters accepted a lucrative invitation to speak at the University of Texas. As the date of his lecture approached, he received a letter from Texas enclosing forms for him to sign. In order to receive his honorarium, he was told, he would have to provide not only his social security number but a statement saying whether he belonged to any organization on the United States attorney general's list of subversive groups. Winters replied that he had not read the attorney general's list, but that he had better cancel the lecture because he had long been a member of two organizations he knew to be unpopular in Texas, the ACLU and the NAACP. At last the authorities at the University of Texas found a way of paying Winters's honorarium and expenses without requiring him to answer the offensive question.

During all his years at Stanford, Winters had never read his poems to a Stanford audience, although the English department and the university annually sponsored at least half a dozen readings by major and minor poets. He had long since bought his life membership in the NAACP, but as I became involved first in some local efforts to end discrimination, and consequently in NAACP membership drives, Winters surprised me one day by offering to read his poems at a benefit for the NAACP. He would not give a reading at Stanford, he said, but he felt so strongly moved by the civil rights campaign that the only purpose for which he would give a reading was an NAACP benefit. That was in 1959, a year or so before the Student Nonviolent Coordinating Committee gained national attention. Winters's reading was a financial success for the NAACP, and a personal triumph. His theory about the oral reading of poetry was as controversial as some of his other critical judgments, but hearing him read some of his own poems in his deep, almost chanting rhythms gave me and many others in that audience an exhilarating appreciation of his method. The local chapter of the NAACP bought Mrs. Winters a life membership with the proceeds of her husband's reading.

In the early 1950s John Loftis was the only member of our department who owned a television set, and even he was able to attribute this anomaly to the unsolicited generosity of his father. Several of us would meet at the Loftis house occasionally to watch a Hallmark-sponsored Shakespearean play. Winters, I remember, went there with us to watch some of the daytime sessions of the Army-McCarthy hearings in 1954. When I bought a television set the next year, Winters expressed interest in some of the championship boxing matches that were then among the most popular athletic contests one could watch at home. He had done some boxing as a young man rebuilding his strength after he had recovered from tuberculosis, and although I later decided that professional boxing was a business too brutally destructive to be regarded as a sport, we shared an admiration for Sugar Ray Robinson and Archie Moore. Winters came to my house several times to watch championship fights during the period when Moore was light-heavyweight champion and Robinson was not only welterweight and middleweight champion but almost won the light-heavyweight title as well. Since these fights were scheduled for prime time in the East, they would end before eight o'clock Pacific time. We would have an early dinner before the fight and Winters would leave soon after the last round, for he observed a strict routine of rising very early in the morning and retiring very early at night.

4

Even in those days when he led a relatively active social life, Yvor and Janet Lewis Winters lived simply. The furniture in their small house in Los Altos did not change in all the years of our association, and Winters drove a 1950 Plymouth Suburban from 1949 until he stopped driving in the year before his death. In his last several years he virtually stopped accepting invitations and entertaining guests at home, although he did like to receive visits from individual friends during the day. In both the early years and the late ones he was a gracious host, whether he cooked and served the meal outdoors in his shaded garden or simply served a glass of bourbon before taking up his accustomed place in the old Morris chair in his living room. At Christmas time he would provide holly and other greenery for decorations for his friends' houses, and as we young colleagues built houses of our own he gave us small bay and loquat trees out of his garden. (When he first offered me a loquat to eat, I asked hesitantly whether it tasted like a kumquat or a peach, or a lemon. He replied, "It tastes like a loquat.")

As he went out less, he would telephone more. For a man who spoke relatively little, he was surprisingly uninhibited in his willingness to telephone. During the years of our closest professional association, from about 1959 to his retirement in 1966, he would often call to discuss departmental affairs, or a dissertation we were both assigned to read, or a publication of my own that I had given him. His comments on both of my books and several of my articles and reviews came to me in this form—partly, I suppose, out of considerate understanding that an author would appreciate having some response to a work soon after a friend had finished reading, but perhaps also because he found it easier to converse over the telephone, when he chose the momentary occasion, than face to face, at a time that had to be arranged and in a situation that could not be so readily terminated. It was during one of these calls that he told me of his encounter with the University of Texas.

When he telephoned me, he always identified himself as Yvor

if my wife answered the phone, but if I happened to answer first he would simply greet me by name and count on me to identify his voice. I never presumed to ask him about the two different names by which people knew him. His full name was Arthur Yvor Winters. He signed his work as Yvor Winters and, so far as I can remember, was addressed by all his Stanford colleagues as Yvor, until one of his former students joined the faculty. But his wife, the students (especially the poets but including the younger Albert Guerard) who had worked closely with him, and old non-academic friends always called him Arthur. This double identity has bothered me only on those occasions, which still occur now and then, that find me conversing about Yvor with someone who continues to call him Arthur. I have not yet ventured to adopt my interlocutor's version of the name, for fear that presumption might be more offensive than confusion.

Although it would be even more presumptuous to comment on Winters's marriage, an incident that occurred in 1980 offers belated testimony about the range of his character. I heard Janet Lewis Winters being interviewed at Stanford as one in a series of women writers. In answer to a question from the audience about the most valuable influences upon her development as a writer, she promptly named her father (director of the Lewis Institute in Chicago) and her husband. But the questioner persisted: "Didn't your husband hold you back? I mean, wouldn't you have been able to write more books if he had helped clean the house and had concentrated on your writing as well as on his own?"

The unexpected reply came instantaneously: "Oh, but of course he did do the housework for years, and he not only edited but typed my novels and poems as well!"

Winters was an unusually responsible colleague even after his eminence had been belatedly recognized by a good salary and an endowed chair. He made up and read the departmental language examinations in French and Spanish; characteristically, he made them up stringently and graded them generously. When he and I were the two readers of the French examinations, he would regularly read them first, indicating the errors in translation by making a small check mark against the margin for each error that occurred in any line of the student's prose. He also submitted questions regularly for the Ph.D. comprehensive examinations and served as a reader of those examinations until his first cancer operation in 1964. For at least a decade I saw and discussed with him a great variety of examinations, and I found him as consistently fair and even as generous as anyone else with whom I shared similar duties. I knew students who trimmed their opinions to please him in his own courses, and others who said that a student had to do so to survive. In the examinations we shared, I saw abundant evidence to contradict such charges. Many students made no concessions to his opinions, beyond reading material that he had assigned and writing intelligently about it. They prospered nonetheless.

Winters sat regularly as an examiner in the three-hour oral examinations. These were scheduled at the student's request, at almost any time in the academic year, but the calendar naturally became quite crowded toward the end of the spring term. In one exhausting period of ten days in May, Winters and I spent six afternoons together, along with a varying roster of colleagues, examining Ph.D. candidates on American literature. In an effort to avoid boring Winters, I tried to refrain from repeating any question I had asked one of the preceding candidates in that unending parade. Winters entertained me by asking all six students precisely the same question: Discuss Edgar Allan Poe's conception of the relationship between melancholy and beauty. Only one of the students answered that question satisfactorily. Both Winters and I were surprised that the later students had not been forewarned of the question, but of course Winters asked all of them many questions that they could answer, and he agreed to pass them all.

The same generosity characterized his behavior in departmental meetings about faculty appointments and promotions. Like many strong figures who have established a distinctive set of principles in an institution, Winters was distressed by his failure to see those principles secured by the appointment of a successor who was committed to them, or at least one whose poetical and critical work could be certified as excellent according to those principles. In the decade before his retirement he tried several times to persuade the department to invite Edgar Bowers or J. V. Cunningham, the poets he admired most, to join the faculty. Eventually Kenneth Fields, a younger poet who had worked closely with Winters, was appointed to an assistant professorship after Winters had retired, and Winters was pleased by the subsequent appointment of Donald Davie. But during the period of Winters's active service and in the first year of his retirement he had no indication that his ideas would be perpetuated at Stanford in advanced classes in the writing of poetry. Believing as he did that several worthy candidates were available if only his colleagues would choose among them, Winters might well have tried to block appointments favored by some of his colleagues in other fields, especially those appointments that would increase what he regarded as the faculty's disproportionate emphasis on modern fiction and either psychoanalytic or impressionistic criticism. He could easily have tried to block several promotions and senior appointments in the seven years of my membership on the committee that made such decisions, but he did not block a single one. He even endorsed for the department chairmanship Thomas C. Moser, whom he might have been expected to oppose as the author of a psychoanalytic study of Joseph Conrad's fiction. And although Winters sent Moser some of his fiercest letters on one issue and another, he concurred with me and most of our colleagues in praising Moser as an extraordinarily humane and perceptive administrator during five of the most contentious years in Stanford's brief history.

Even at Stanford, of course, Winters's influence could not be measured solely by whether Wintersians were appointed to the faculty. Irving Howe provided one amusing illustration of that influence when he reviewed in the *New York Review of Books* the Oxford University Press edition of Frederick Goddard Tuckerman's collected poems. The book, edited by N. Scott Momaday, with an introduction by Yvor Winters, was published two years after

Howe's departure from Stanford. Howe had read it as a member of Momaday's dissertation committee in 1962. Without mentioning that connection, or his delighted surprise at how well prepared he had found some Stanford undergraduates to read poetry, Howe's review encloses a serious discussion of Tuckerman's poetry in a familiar frame: the eccentric judgments of Yvor Winters. Howe speaks respectfully of Winters, but his just reminder that Witter Bynner was one of the first modern readers to praise Tuckerman plays to the sophisticated reader's awareness of Winters's reputation. As if Howe and we had all known some of Tuckerman's best poems right along, he says he hopes we will not have to suffer "the vulgarity of a revival." He challenges Winters's claim that Tuckerman's "The Cricket" is the greatest poem written in English in the nineteenth century, and he claims the middle ground —a secure resting place between Winters's exaggerated praise and the public's neglect—in solid praise for a few of Tuckerman's sonnets. He does not report—perhaps he did not know—that those sonnets include the very ones Winters regularly singled out in assigning Tuckerman's poems to graduate students, including the student who helped Howe to choose the poems for an anthology of nineteenth-century American literature.

5

My purpose here is to testify that despite his strong judgments and feelings Winters was usually a responsible, generous, and flexible colleague. The truth of this generalization does not require me to deny that he also had a powerful temper, whose severity some of his colleagues, and especially the chairman, occasionally experienced. Not all of his letters to colleagues were about how to build a whelping box; some concerned how *not* to build a university faculty or curriculum in English and American literature. Although I never received one of these letters, I saw two or three examples. Like some of the severe pronouncements in Winters's criticism, these denunciations gained impact from his superb control of his rhetoric. Just as the intensity of his passion must sometimes have moved his fingers over keys that expressed more anger than the occasion deserved, so his perfect ear for the language and his scorn of circumlocution must occasionally have brought reasonable indignation closer to the sound of fury.

One of our few conversations about his own essays gave me a rare glimpse not only of the biographical significance in Winters's vehemently antiromantic criticism, but also of his self-knowledge. I often heard him laugh heartily at humor in literature and in conversation, and he often joined in witty banter that placed him and his interlocutors in a circle of privileged vulnerability to retorts, but I cannot remember that I ever heard him really laugh at himself. His response to a question about his essay on Hart Crane therefore had especial meaning to me. Some time in the early 1960s I reread that essay, "The Significance of *The Bridge; . . .* or, What Are We to Think of Professor X?," and I asked Winters to explain the ethical reasoning behind the concluding paragraph. There Winters declares a strong preference for Crane, "a saint of the wrong religion," the misguided genius whose willingness to act out his pernicious principles damaged other human beings, wasted his own literary gifts, and destroyed his life. Winters has just deplored that waste, but he insists that he prefers Crane to the professors of literature who, though they profess the same self-indulgent romantic principles, lead conventional lives themselves.

Although I had not then heard Winters's remark about the man who was sincerely full of banana oil, my question implied the same criticism of Winters's preference for Crane, who had "the courage of his convictions, the virtue of integrity." I could see the justice in scorning genteel hypocrisy or philosophical inconsistency, but I asked why one *ought* to prefer an actively destructive person to a responsible citizen whose actual behavior did not live down to the destructive tendencies of his principles. Winters's answer was as brief as some of the others I have recorded here. "You forget," he said, "that I once nearly fell into that romantic world." There ended the discussion. I now take Winters's comment as an allusion to the experience recounted later, in his preface to *The Early Poems of Yvor Winters,* an allusion to his own belated discovery that commitment to free verse and "associational" images is at last not liberating but tyrannously restrictive. What I believe he conceded in our brief exchange was the persistence of an allegiance he could not rationally justify. Both the power of his remembered attraction to romantic or at least experimental views of the artist's vocation, and the even stronger power of his revulsion from the consequences of those views, were perceptible in his essay and in our conversation about it. He does not merely joke when he declares that he would "gladly emulate Odysseus, if I could, and go down to the shadows for another hour's conversation with Crane on the subject of poetry; whereas, politeness permitting, I seldom go out of my way to discuss poetry with Professor X."

In the last four or five years before his retirement, Winters gave up some of his old courses. For twenty years he had taught a course called Representative American Novelists, because he believed the curriculum would otherwise neglect them, but he had told me (quoting himself) that novels are for the very young. He was happy to reduce the range of that course from seven novelists to two, Hawthorne and Melville, and in 1961 he gladly surrendered to a new young colleague Hawthorne and Melville, along with the harpoon that he annually carried to one lecture on *Moby-Dick*. When he stopped teaching his seminar on American historians, he gave me his valuable edition of Henry Adams's *History of the United States During the Administrations of Thomas Jefferson and James Madison*. When he stopped teaching James Fenimore Cooper, he gave me his set of Cooper's novels, an edition that had no commercial value beyond what Winters's own characteristic notes—check marks in the margins and page numbers inside the front cover—might one day give them. Coming across some of those check marks in the texts that I have read since receiving the very useful gift, I have often been reminded of Winters's remark a year or two before his retirement, that if he had to choose between rereading Cooper and rereading Hawthorne now, he would choose Cooper.

But of course he was rereading neither one. In his last years as a teacher his professional actions endorsed the reasoning behind his insistence that novels were for the young. He tried to concentrate on the subjects that were most important to him, the essential things, great poems, central principles; and he left subordinate genres to those who might still be interested in the details of experience. Ever since his early thirties, when he had written a poem describing himself precociously as a middle-aged teacher of "Corrosion and distrust, / Exacting what I must," he had enjoyed declaring that he would now devote his declining years to the English lyric, and in his last two years of active teaching, after an operation for cancer of the tongue had threatened to prevent him from teaching or uttering his favorite poems, he at last had the opportunity to restrict his energy to the history of English and American poetry and to working with a few graduate students whom he had chosen for fellowships in the writing of poetry. The Stanford English department recognized this winnowing process by publishing in honor of his retirement a small volume of twenty-five poems, one of his favorites (so far as Helen Pinkerton Trimpi, who edited the book, could identify them) by each of twenty-five poets who had worked with him at some time during his four decades as a poet and critic. The title of the volume came from the last line of Winters's poem *On Teaching the Young:*

> The poet's only bliss
> Is in cold certitude,
> Laurel, archaic, rude.

Winters's retirement party, which he agreed to attend on condition that there be no speeches, was the last occasion on which his friends and associates were allowed to assemble to honor him. He accepted the surprise gift graciously and seemed to take much pleasure in it. But he continued his recent practice of virtual withdrawal from social life, except for receiving brief visits from friends who would call on him at his house during the day. In order to finish *Forms of Discovery,* his critical history of the lyric in English and American literature, he postponed a second cancer operation, and the metastasis progressed rapidly after he did submit to the operation.

I visited him several times during his last few months. To replace the dead Airedales who in life had been so intimidating to visitors that Winters would lock them away before opening the front door, he had now acquired an English bulldog puppy. This powerful little beast liked to hurl her front shoulders against a visitor's legs, and she would not desist until her master took her into his lap. Her persistence reminded me of Jim Smiley's hilarious dog in Mark Twain's story of the celebrated frog, and I was moved by Winters's hearty laughter, solemn though he usually was in these months, when I read him the familiar tale of the bulldog who always won wagers for his owner by clamping his jaws onto the opposing dog's hind leg and hanging on until the other dog quit. My last memory of Winters includes Roxy the bulldog, relaxed in his lap. Winters himself seems to be waiting with a resigned tenacity for the death that he has long ago made up his mind to recognize as annihilation. He has grown a handsome white beard, and wears a flannel mantle, to cover the surgical scars. He has lost a great part of his bulky weight, and he has lost his voice. But he can still whisper his brief, decisive answers, he has told the doctor that there must be no last-minute heroics, and he has decreed that there must be no funeral or memorial service.

Sarah K. Marker

TO FIGHT ALOUD IS VERY BRAVE

I can still see the late Sarah Marker, Pat's unmarried aunt, in her last embattled days as the proprietor of Marker's Confectionery in Reedsville, Pennsylvania. She does not use the wheelchair. It is folded against the wall near the ice-cream packer, the wheels and frame shining like nothing else in her store. The chair she sits in is of a dirty green, its tiny wheels invisible, its torn seat protected from her bulk by a thick pad of stained, corrugated foam rubber. By lifting her bandaged right leg off the floor and propelling her chair with her left foot, she can move laboriously about the store, and even to the bathroom in her adjoining house, but for most of the day she sits absolutely still behind the cash register. There she has built her little fortification, and there she sits, a sentry without relief, for fifteen hours a day.

I never tired, during my semiannual visits, of observing how the townspeople had learned to wait on themselves. A customer who wanted a pack of cigarettes would enter briskly, step behind the long counters filled with what used to be called penny candy, remove a pack of cigarettes, cross the store to take a bottle of Pepsi-Cola from the refrigerator, a loaf of bread from the free-standing bread counter, and a *Police Gazette* from the magazine stand. (She did not sell *Playboy* or any of the newer slick magazines, but she always had a good supply, at least since her mother's death, of *True Confessions* and the other pulps.) Then he would come to the counter to pay up. "Well, Sarah," he would say—

even the children call her Sarah, though she is over eighty now—"Looks as if State better hire a new *football* coach if Paterno can't make 'em play no better'n that. Why they almost *lost* that game yesterday."

In my memory she nods and says, "Yes, I believe that's true." Except for her long months in the isolation ward of the hospital, when the doctors were threatening to amputate her leg, she attended every home game at Penn State for twenty years after 1959, her fortieth homecoming. After 1977 she went to the games less uncomfortably, letting Jack Orth lift her wheelchair into the trunk of Reddy, her 1949 Buick. The last time she insisted on walking to her seat, when Pat and I drove up from Virginia for the Stanford game in 1977, the nickel-size calluses on the soles of her feet hurt so badly that she had to gasp at nearly every step, even while letting her walker shift much of the weight to her arms. The walk from the parking lot to her seat on the forty-five-yard line took more than an hour. At the end of that game Pat took charge; she simply ordered one of the men at the first-aid station to bring a wheelchair to carry Sarah back to her car, and Sarah went without a word. Pat and I could not decide whether Sarah had acquiesced because she had recognized the reality of her pain or because she could not bear to keep the store closed for the extra hour it would have taken her to walk to her car. The store, we agreed, was her life. She insisted that she wanted to die there, and she would not choose the other death that we and the other relatives kept urging on her. She would not sell the store and move to a Home.

On the counter beside the old register she kept a column of cans of Skoal, "the smokeless tobacco," and an open carton of Marlboros, her fastest-selling brand of cigarettes, for the customers she didn't know, the few who came to her to be served. If she felt unusually tired, she would even send one of those strangers behind the counter when he asked for a less popular brand—unless a loitering neighbor happened to be there to serve him. But she herself took all the money and gave all the change.

Her register was just an old adding machine, long ago broken so that the tape registered nothing when someone pushed the keys and pulled down the arm. For the state sales tax she kept a stack of tops from cigarette cartons, which she covered with long columns tallying her receipts. She kept one- and five-dollar bills in the open drawer of the old machine, but the coins for change came from smooth round wells in an oak drawer below the counter. Customers who watched closely might perceive an even deeper layer. In a lower drawer under the counter stood a green plastic pouch. Here she slipped in the tens and twenties, and she stacked the Kennedy half-dollars in the drawer beside the pouch.

All these receptacles stood open. The drawers under the counter were too heavy and deep for her to open and close, and the drawer of the register no longer had any connection to the lever that used to open it while ringing up the total on the tape. Dust, corn chips, and remnants of other old snacks gave the open drawers a film of grease and grit around the money. From the green pouch on Mondays and Thursdays she paid cash for the weekly supply brought in and set up for display by the bread man and milkman, and under the pouch she kept receipts for these transactions during her last forty years.

Ever since the third robbery, she had hidden less money around the house. Oh, we would find an occasional cache even in the final days, a mixing bowl full of quarters and dimes in the oven. But the third robbery persuaded her at last that it was better to let the banker know how much money she had than to let hoodlums carry it off. The earlier robbers had angered her without frightening her. The first pair had been mere burglars, young boys who broke a window and were after cigarettes and some change. She was sure she knew who they were, although she couldn't prove it. Well, they hadn't even come through the open door between the store and the house. Lying on her cot within a few feet of that door, she had heard the glass fall when they broke a pane to unlock the window, but they had escaped, giggling and stumbling, before the police arrived.

The second group were burly thugs, but they did not harm her.

One of them, wearing a stocking over his face, pushed open the unlatched door between store and house, and without the slightest pause walked, as if familiar with the room, directly to her bed. While his two henchmen were ransacking the drawers of her desk, he put his knee on her chest and pressed his open hand against her face, pushing the back of her head so deep into the feather pillow that she could feel the outline of the green pouch. Lying absolutely still, and staring up past his sweaty fingers, she hoped that his other hand would not reach under the pillow, and she concentrated (she told us later) on resisting the impulse to lift her head. At a signal from the others, who had apparently found a leather bag of coins, the knee left her chest, the hand went away from her face, and all three men had left the building before she was able to make her toothless, panting speech intelligible to the police.

That time she had been able to reach the telephone beside her cot, although she had not dared to reach a little farther for her teeth. She knew that if she fell out of bed again she would have to wait till morning to be helped to her feet. Charles Smyser had one of her keys in his service station across the street, and Dick Drager, the bread man, would have him open the front door and check the floor of the house if the door was still locked at seven o'clock in the morning. Once Sarah had simply slid off the high stool at her kitchen sink; the stool had given way as she had begun to lower her bulk onto what she had mistaken for the center of the seat. Hitting the front edge of the seat instead, her hips had slid down along the legs until she ended up sitting on the floor. At first she had laughed too hard to be able to find the wind to lift herself up, and then she had tried soberly three or four times before she resigned herself to leaning back and waiting the twelve hours till morning. It took at least two men to get her onto her feet, and Charles Smyser prudently employed three, one on each upper arm and one bracing her feet and steadying the walker to accept the weight of her arms as soon as she had been brought upright.

On the morning after the third robbery, all Charles Smyser had to do was call an ambulance. He found her lying on the floor, her head in blood and her hips in urine; these robbers had knocked her on the head while she was counting the day's receipts, and they had found not only the green pouch (which they emptied and discarded) but the family Bible, some money in a mattress upstairs, a small diamond ring, and a pearl necklace. Since they had cut the telephone wires, she could not have summoned the police even if she had been wide awake.

After the robbery she made regular deposits in the bank. She had no clear estimate of the treasure that remained upstairs, for she had not been up there for years, not since the ulcerated sores on her leg began to send out red streaks, across the calf and up toward the knee. When she returned from that month in the isolation ward, she set up her cot in the alcove under the stairway. There the policeman found her when he got Charles Smyser's key and entered the house, sloshing through the flooded store on the night the creek overflowed. He brought her wheelchair to the bed and told her that all houses along the banks had to be evacuated. She refused to go. She told him to tend to the other people; she had never left there in fifty-five years, and she was not going to run away now. Only when he said that if she was determined to stay in that bed he was going to have to climb in there with her, only then did she let him help her into the wheelchair.

Back to the hospital she went after the flood, without even stopping in at the store. She was only seventy-nine then, but in no condition to clear out that muck or to bring her bandages into contact with it. She let her eighty-one-year-old brother, Pat's father, worry about it. It served Merrel right, she said, and she never did thank him when his ailing wife telephoned long distance several weeks later and insisted that he return home. After all, if he hadn't gone off with Eleanor as a missionary to Persia right after he graduated from the seminary in 1921, he might have been called to a church near Reedsville, and Sarah might not have been condemned to work all her life in the store and to clothe his children for him all through the Depression. Now that Mother and Father were gone, and his own children grown and scattered all over the country, he could just come home for a while and keep the family store going.

Of course he had come. He hated the store, its filthy floor and its dirty magazines, the mass of cartons in the storeroom and the stacks of cigarettes, cigars, and chewing tobacco on display. Not even the beloved smell of Lebanon bologna, remembered from childhood and fresh enough to compete with less welcome odors now, could overcome his reluctance. But since the store was literally his sister's home, from which there was no way of detaching her house, he told me that he just had to help her recover from the flood. Right at the time of the Watergate scandal, then, with two hired women working alongside him to scrape down the mud to the ordinary stuff that had made the floor look extraordinarily dirty even before the flood, he found himself laundering money.

The water had come up to the second shelf of a storage cabinet, fourteen inches above the floor, leaving a thick layer of sludge on one of Sarah's legendary stacks of paper money. Merrel agonized over keeping so much money in the house overnight, but the bank manager insisted that the bills would have to be cleaned before they could be accepted for deposit. Merrel dumped the bills into a net bag, the kind used for protecting lingerie in washing machines, and ran it through a hot-water cycle in Sarah's machine. He shook the clean, wrinkled bills into a small carton and, after an anxious night, took them to the bank first thing in the morning, but the manager snorted that he could not accept all those crumpled bills. Merrel took them back to the store. One of the women waited on customers, and he himself pressed the bills with Sarah's steam iron. Then, while his sister lay unaware in the hospital fifteen miles away, he won the victory for which she never did forgive him, not even after the robbers' assault had persuaded her to put her money in the bank.

He told me that he went through the entire house looking for the money. He found bills everywhere: under the bowl of artificial fruit, in birthday cards dated February 23, 1927, and even in the copy of *Main Street* that he had given her for Christmas in 1921. There he found a twenty-dollar bill, but most of the money was in ones, fives, tens, and coins. He found forty-two silver dollars in a paper bag stuffed in a tin labeled SUGAR. He got out an old Gladstone bag, filled it with the money, snapped it shut, and grabbed the handle. But he could not lift the bag an inch off the floor. He strapped two of Sarah's old belts around the bag for support and called Vera out of the store to help him. Together they staggered toward the bank three blocks away. The people who greeted them didn't seem to understand what the burden was until the breathless pair, each with hands clasped under the bag, turned in at the bank. Merrel rented a safe deposit box in Sarah's name and asked that the coins be put in it. He did not even take time to count the rest of the cash. He told the manager to count the money, credit it to Sarah's account, and send a receipt or deposit slip. He and Vera were back at the store within forty minutes of their departure.

When he gave Sarah the receipts at the hospital the next day, he told us, she was furious. "Never you mind how I was going to protect it," she said. "Those were my private belongings. You had no right."

Sitting out there on the edge of the highway, with the threshold scarcely one step above the level of the road, the building invited robbers, and Merrel knew that her immobility and the rumors of hidden cash made it all the more vulnerable. Yet he said that he did feel the touch of sympathetic shame when he saw some of the sights that his search had inevitably exposed, and we understood some of his feelings when we had to go through her things after her death. Whatever she thought of his challenge to her stewardship of her property, he knew that the violation of her privacy was worse. She wouldn't care about his seeing the quilts their mother had sewn, with the neat signature embroidered on every one and "the Depression Year, 1933" on her favorite. Those were for his daughters anyway. Nor was it all those flat boxes of handkerchiefs, each packed away with its gift card in the cedar chest after the box had been opened and the thank-you note sent at Christmas or her birthday. No, it must have been the trousseau, the hope chest, we decided years after he had refrained from telling us—the trousseau must have struck him as the worst. Not so much the size 54 bloomers and green silk polka-dot pajamas or the embroidered linen sheets, as the very idea that she had given such material nourishment to ordinary hopes. He told us that although he would act no differently if he had to decide all over again, he agreed that he had no right.

I can only imagine Aunt Sarah on her last day in the store. She would be waiting for Patrick Kavanaugh, who shuffled in every morning at nine o'clock to watch the Donahue show, and she would be glad for the company, although she disliked the show as heartily as the Kavanaugh sister who refused to allow it in the house. Forty years ago Sarah could not have imagined sitting beside a man while watching an interview of a father whom a surgeon had transformed into a woman. (Forty years ago nobody would have performed the operation, or dreamed of staging the interview.) Forty years ago Sherman Warner might have taken one of his new Oldsmobiles for a spin before putting it on the showroom floor, and he might have asked her to ride on up with him to the dairy at State College for an ice-cream cone. She often told us that if she had married Sherman Warner when he asked her, he might not then have been stricken dead while moving her bales of Sunday papers into her store. For she would have sold the store and moved into Sherman's house in Lewistown.

The last time that I saw Mr. Kavanaugh come into the store, he complained that it was too dark, and he asked Pat to put some drops in his eye. He tilted his head back and cautioned her: "Only one drop in each eye now." He held one eye open, then the other, as Pat released the drops. He blinked, thanked her, and glided shuffling behind the cash register to watch the television. He carried all his valuable papers and his favorite mementos on his person, for fear they would be stolen by someone in his sister's house. "I have bad neighbors," he told us. Before leaving the store, he offered to show me the identification badge from his years at the Standard Steel Works, where he had been welding before I was born, and he reminded me that his wage there had been as low as seventy-five cents for a twelve-hour day.

On Sarah's last day, young Fleda came in to help before the nurse arrived. I can see the scene as clearly as if I were watching it on the tube in Charlottesville. While Sarah trundles her chair to the bathroom for her mid-morning relief, Fleda scrubs a six-foot-square section of the floor behind the cash register. The visiting nurse has threatened to stop coming and to have Sarah packed off to the hospital if the filthy conditions are not cleaned up; by an unsatisfactory compromise Sarah has agreed to have the floor under the ailing foot washed twice a week.

When Sarah calls from the bathroom, Fleda enters the house to stand behind the swivel chair. Sarah has the green pouch in her teeth. Groaning, she presses down on the fleecy sole of her slipper and the heel of her bandaged foot, heaves her hips upward as she bears down on the arm rests beside her toilet, and rises trembling from the seat. As she twists her body ninety degrees, so that her back faces the open doorway, Fleda deftly presses the front seat of the chair against the back of Sarah's legs. With a great gasp of pain and relief, Sarah manages to bend her knees and drop into the chair, with Fleda braced firmly (as I have sometimes been) against the back, and Fleda's left hand snatches the pouch just as Sarah's teeth release it, while the body is still subsiding into the chair.

The wheezing and the panting will not stop until just before the nurse arrives. It was when I saw how much effort it took Aunt Sarah to get up from her chair and onto the walker that Pat and I made our most impassioned plea for selling out. Either because Sarah could not bear the pain of pressure on her calluses, or because her knees could no longer shift so much weight, rising from her chair had become a heroic achievement, and I realized when I actually watched it that she must have been unsure of the outcome every time she dared to make the effort. I saw it in her fingers and her forearms. She dug all eight fingers into the underside of the oak counter behind her cash register. I could see her forearms tremble as she rose slowly out of the chair, and, especially in the moments of suspense when it seemed that her knees might not succeed in shifting her center of gravity, that she might sink back into the chair, I felt myself cheering her spirit onward and upward. She breathed in gasps so rapid, yet with so many little groans, that I first feared a coronary or stroke and then almost wished for a swift, fatal one.

On the day after Sarah's death, the nurse told us Sarah had been calm and that the leg had looked a little better. "She said she had a surprise for me, that picture of herself in the red dress, with the gold frame. She said it was her Christmas present to all of you, a few weeks late."

And there Sarah sits, in the picture as she did in stubborn life. She did not quite die here in her store, as she had hoped to do even as she had fought to survive. When the attack struck her that night, she let them take her to the intensive care unit to keep her heart going and to ease her pain. But they did not insist on trying to insert a pacemaker through the collapsed vein. The copies of her picture had already been mailed to us in Virginia, and to the five nieces in the Middle West and West, and to their eleven children, and to her brother. For many of us this image will replace our own fading memories. Some will remember the eighty-six-year-old sentry seated at her post, rather than the fat, lively, humorous character some of us knew long ago.

But those who flew east or drove north to her funeral found that, except for the stolen family Bible, she had faithfully protected the living record entrusted to her. Every letter, post card, birthday card, and photograph that came into the household in the last hundred years could be found in one of the cartons cluttering the dining room. Letters home from France in 1918, from Persia in the twenties, from colleges in Ohio in the forties. Thank-you notes from nieces for wool suits sewn by their grandmother in the forties and for Easter and Halloween candy sent to their children by Sarah in the fifties and sixties. While Pat and I were down at the funeral home learning that Sarah had not really paid all her expenses in advance but that her savings would easily pay for the exorbitant cost of an oversized coffin and vault, Pat's sister found in the house the list of townspeople who had contributed twenty-five cents, fifty cents, two dollars in 1898, to help Sarah's father buy the supplies to open the store, after his right hand, mangled in a mishap at the axe factory, had been amputated. Pat found among the quilts patches from shirts that she remembers having ironed during her summer visits in the thirties. By some obscure association these brought back the sound of Sarah's snores as Pat (aged seven) lay beside her in the double bed, resisting sleep for fear of being smothered if the fat aunt should roll over. Pat remembered too how the bed shook on the night that Sarah, having dared to conceal a farting bladder under the cushion of Grandfather's dining room chair, had dared to laugh only after she came to bed three hours later.

For decades Sarah had been telling us that she had prepaid all her funeral expenses, even for the flowers, and that she would never draw up a will, because she wanted to sit up there in heaven and watch us fight over her money. As we reminisced on the day of her funeral, we marveled at the generous will she did execute: whom did she trust to take it up to the bank and set it on top of the silver dollars in the safe deposit box? And of course we agreed that the aunt who once took pride in being the fattest woman in the county would find amusement in requiring an enormous coffin, and in the ridiculous imitation of green grass covering her open grave on a day when every eye would be dazzled by the sunlight on eight inches of fresh snow.

No new stone was needed. Her grave is beside her mother's and father's, and that of the brother who died in infancy eighty years ago. When the family had once again dispersed, the letters and photographs scattered among the nieces, the house and the store were sold. The swollen cans of applesauce, which Patrick Kavanaugh was almost allowed to buy one day until Pat Levin's acute perception saved him, were discarded at last. Sarah never did carry out her promise to open one, taste the contents, and rule on their condition. The cartons of puffed rice in the storeroom, undermined by mice so neatly that we could not perceive the loss until we picked up a new box to replenish a shelf in the store, were also thrown out, along with the wormy and stale candy and the spoiled baby food. The forgetful lawyer whom Sarah named as executor because she had taught him English in the sixth grade in 1920 did actually file the will for probate. But none of us ever did learn by what ill-considered or malicious remark an official at the local polls in the presidential election of 1924 offended Sarah so deeply that she never voted again.